'CLINICAL GUIDE OF PSYCHIATRIC NURSING'

DR ANAND LINGESWARAN

Made with ♥ on the Notion Press Platform
www.notionpress.com

This book is dedicated to all undergraduate and postgraduate psychiatric nursing students and nursing teachers who have chosen the noble path of mental health care. Your dedication, empathy, and perseverance in understanding and treating mental disorders inspire hope and healing for those in need.

To the mental health professionals who tirelessly advocate for compassionate and evidence-based care, your work transforms lives and strengthens communities.

And to the patients and their families, whose courage and resilience remind us of the profound impact of compassionate psychiatric nursing—this guide is a tribute to you.

May this book serve as a valuable resource in your journey toward excellence in clinical psychiatric care.

Contents

Foreword

Mental health care is a cornerstone of holistic well-being, and psychiatric nursing plays a vital role in ensuring quality care for individuals with mental disorders. As the prevalence of mental health conditions continues to rise globally, the need for well-trained psychiatric nursing professionals has never been more critical.

'Clinical Guide of Psychiatric Nursing' is a timely and comprehensive resource designed to bridge the gap between theoretical knowledge and practical application. This guide provides an in-depth understanding of the diagnosis, management, and evidence-based interventions for commonly encountered mental health disorders. It is meticulously structured to equip postgraduate nursing students with the skills necessary to deliver compassionate, ethical, and effective care in various clinical settings.

The authors have carefully curated this guide to serve as both an academic reference and a clinical companion. Each chapter is thoughtfully crafted, incorporating the latest advancements in psychiatric nursing, case-based scenarios, and practical strategies to enhance clinical decision-making. The content is aligned with contemporary psychiatric nursing education, ensuring that students are well-prepared to meet the challenges of real-world mental health care.

This book stands as a testament to the commitment of psychiatric nursing educators and practitioners who strive to enhance mental health services through knowledge and skill development. It is a valuable addition to postgraduate psychiatric nursing education and will undoubtedly serve as a trusted resource for students, educators, and healthcare professionals alike.

I commend the authors for their dedication to advancing psychiatric nursing practice and for creating a guide that will shape the future of mental health care. May this book inspire confidence, competence, and compassionate care among all who use it.

Dr. Anand Lingeswaran

Professor of Psychiatry

ANIIMS

29/01/2025

Preface

Mental health care is an evolving field that demands both scientific knowledge and compassionate practice. As postgraduate psychiatric nursing students step into this crucial domain, they require a strong foundation in the assessment, diagnosis, and management of common mental disorders. This book, ''Clinical Guide of Psychiatric Nursing', serves as a comprehensive resource tailored to bridge the gap between theoretical understanding and practical application in psychiatric nursing.

Designed to meet the needs of postgraduate nursing students specializing in psychiatry, this guide provides a structured approach to understanding prevalent mental disorders, including their etiology, clinical features, diagnostic criteria, and evidence-based treatment strategies. The content is aligned with contemporary psychiatric nursing practices and integrates key aspects of psychopharmacology, psychotherapy, and holistic patient care.

The book is organized into sections that systematically cover a range of mental health conditions, such as mood disorders, anxiety disorders, psychotic disorders, substance use disorders, and neurodevelopmental conditions. Each chapter includes clinical scenarios, case discussions, and practical interventions to enhance critical thinking and clinical decision-making skills.

In addition to its academic value, this guide emphasizes a patient-centered approach, highlighting the importance of empathy, ethical considerations, and cultural competence in psychiatric nursing practice. The role of psychiatric nurses as advocates, educators, and caregivers is explored in depth, ensuring that students are well-equipped to provide high-quality mental health care in diverse clinical settings.

This book is the result of extensive research and practical experience in the field of mental health nursing. It is intended to be a valuable companion for postgraduate nursing students, educators, and professionals striving to enhance their competence in psychiatric care.

We hope that this guide will inspire students to approach mental health nursing with dedication, empathy, and a commitment to lifelong learning. May it serve as a useful reference in their journey toward becoming skilled psychiatric nursing professionals who make a meaningful difference in the lives of individuals with mental health disorders.

Dr. Anand Lingeswaran
Professor of Psychiatry
2025

Acknowledgements

I express my sincere gratitude to everyone who contributed to the development of this book, 'Clinical Guide of Psychiatric Nursing'. This book is the result of extensive research, clinical experience, and the support of many individuals who have been instrumental in shaping its content.

First and foremost, I extend my deepest appreciation to my mentors and colleagues in the field of psychiatric nursing and mental health care. Their guidance, expertise, and encouragement have been invaluable in ensuring the accuracy and relevance of this guide. I am particularly grateful to [Mentor's Name] for their unwavering support and insightful feedback throughout the writing process.

I would also like to acknowledge the postgraduate psychiatric nursing students and practitioners whose curiosity, dedication, and passion for mental health care inspired this work. Their commitment to learning and improving patient outcomes has been a driving force behind the creation of this guide.

A heartfelt thank you to my family and friends for their patience, understanding, and encouragement during the countless hours spent researching and writing. Their unwavering support has been my greatest strength.

Lastly, I am grateful to the publishers and editorial team for their dedication in bringing this book to fruition. Their professionalism and expertise have played a crucial role in refining the content and making it accessible to readers.

I hope this guide serves as a valuable resource for postgraduate psychiatric nursing students, enhancing their knowledge and confidence in providing compassionate and effective mental health care.

Dr. Anand Lingeswaran
Professor of Psychiatry
ANIIMS

Prologue

Mental health care is a dynamic and ever-evolving field, requiring both a deep understanding of psychiatric disorders and the ability to apply evidence-based clinical interventions. For postgraduate psychiatric nursing students, mastering the principles of mental health care is not just an academic pursuit but a crucial step toward becoming skilled and compassionate practitioners.

This book, 'Clinical Guide of Psychiatric Nursing', is designed to serve as a comprehensive resource, bridging theoretical knowledge with practical clinical applications. It provides a structured approach to understanding, diagnosing, and managing prevalent psychiatric conditions encountered in diverse healthcare settings.

The complexity of mental health disorders demands a holistic perspective—one that integrates biological, psychological, and social factors. This book emphasizes patient-centered care, therapeutic communication, and the ethical and professional responsibilities of psychiatric nurses. Each chapter covers key mental health disorders, including mood disorders, anxiety disorders, psychotic disorders, substance use disorders, and neurocognitive conditions, among others. The guide includes evidence-based assessment tools, treatment modalities, pharmacological considerations, and case-based discussions to enhance clinical decision-making skills.

As mental health continues to gain recognition as a vital component of overall well-being, psychiatric nurses play an increasingly significant role in delivering quality care. This book aims to empower postgraduate students with the knowledge, confidence, and critical thinking abilities needed to navigate the complexities of psychiatric nursing. Whether working in hospitals, community settings, or specialized mental health facilities, this guide serves as a reliable companion on the journey to becoming a proficient mental health practitioner.

Through dedication, empathy, and a commitment to lifelong learning, psychiatric nurses can profoundly impact the lives of individuals facing mental health challenges. This book is a step toward that goal, equipping students with the essential clinical insights to provide compassionate, effective, and evidence-based mental health care.

Welcome to a journey of professional growth and excellence in psychiatric nursing.

CONTENTS

CHAPTER I

MEDICAL AND PSYCHIATRIC ETHICS

Irrespective of any professional medical background, all medical, allied health professionals must adhere to the below mentioned lifesaving ethical principles that will ensure good quality medical service at all times.

<u>Basic Medical Ethical Principles</u>

1. **SAFETY:** Absolutely ensure safety during patient care and treatment first and never indulge in risky unsupervised and unauthorized medical or nursing practice. Check and ensure that you are protected with appropriate legal medical indemnity when you practice your profession.
2. **NON-MALEFICENCE:** Learn to avoid risks or harm to the patient and others involved in the care of the patient. Never indulge in medical misadventure. Doing no harm comes first before learning when to do good or practice your skills.
3. **BENEFICENCE:** Practice skills and provide treatment and care that you have been trained, qualified, accredited by the appropriate accrediting organization.
4. **JUSTICE:** As a medical professional you must always strive to provide the best possible treatment and care to your patients at all times and practice your skills appropriately under supervision if necessary. Personal gains of any kind must never interfere with patient care.

In both instances 3 & 4, if unsure, you must learn and practice to seek help and ask for help from colleagues and supervisors always. ASK, SEEK HELP...

<u>Specific Psychiatric Ethical Principles</u>

I. ENSURING PRIVACY AND CONFIDENTIALITY: More than other patients, patients with mental illness may be very concerned about the need for confidentiality of their clinical and personal information because of stigma and discrimination and so nursing staff must be very mindful of the same at all times during patient care. The psychiatric nurse must attempt to build a genuine and professional patient- nurse relationship. Often, people with mental illness tend to connect better with their nurses and may cooperate in adhering to prescribed treatment.

Exceptions to this clause can be patients who are expressing dangerous intention to harm his/her treating medical staff, family, friends or public directly due to the nature of the symptoms of their mental illness, cases of disclosure of child abuse under the POSH Act. Patients can express serious intentions to harm themselves by suicide and this information cannot be considered confidential by the nurse. In both these circumstances, nurses must be very careful and document the risk behaviour to self or others as expressed by the patient and bring it to the attention of the treating psychiatrist at the earliest. In these cases, safety to life must be given precedence over confidentiality of disclosed information.

II. MAINTAINING THERAPEUTIC BOUNDARIES: The clinical interaction of nurses with their patients is usually more intimate and of longer time duration in comparison to doctors, and this gives them a greater opportunity to establish a therapeutic relationship with the patients, family or friends. Researchers say that it becomes difficult for nurses to maintain their professional boundaries with their patients especially in the mental health context due to the nature of nursing care provided. Obtaining personal information for clinical purposes only may not be easy as sometimes the medical professional also may share his/her personal information as a persuading method with patients who are not comfortable talking to strangers.

This struggle to maintain a healthy boundary with the patient requires years of training experience with different types of mentally ill people, especially those with difficult personality types. Serious violations of therapeutic boundary with patients could be sexual encounters, exchange of gifts, financial benefits, and non-clinical relationships of any kind. It is again safe for nurses to be mindful of not violating or crossing their professional boundaries when interacting with patients always.

III. INDIVIDUAL, RELIGIOUS AND CULTURAL SENSITIVITY: Despite all the advances in psychiatry, the opinion and perspectives of people with a culture and outside tend to be highly variable and as a medical professional, nurses must be able to acknowledge and understand these important elements that can influence a patient's adherence to the prescribed treatment. Patients may believe in the role of black-magic, witchcraft and one should not ridicule such beliefs during clinical interaction. Beliefs in alternate forms of medicine must be welcomed and the patient must be allowed to make their own decision in their treatment. Poor understanding of a patient's belief system and values may appear as lack of cooperation to

prescribed treatment and the nurse may not understand how to deal with it unless they are open minded. A sincere discussion with patients on their understanding of why mental illness occur, what treatments are available in their culture, and how they wish to include their methods in the current treatment will make it easy for the nurse to convince their patients to take the right treatment.

For example, it may not be wrong for the patient to pray to their deities out of faith while they are receiving treatment in a mental health hospital. The nurses should encourage such practices that are healthy and will improve the outcome of treatment. At the same time, it is not at all advisable for the nursing staff to impose their own religious, cultural values and beliefs on their patients.

Conclusion

The above ethical elements must always be adhered by all medical and paramedical professionals at all times in their interaction with patients during provision of treatment and care. These ethical elements shall protect both the parties from majority of the common medicolegal issues. Ethical principles are the backbone of good standard of medical practice globally. As a member of this medical team, the nurse must always recognize, show responsibility towards ethics in their duties at all times.

CHAPTER II

MENTAL HEALTH ACT, 2017

All mental health professionals must become aware of and utilise the Mental Health

Act of 2017 in their routine clinical practice of psychiatry.

The following Act of Parliament received the assent of the President of India on 7

April 2017 and has been in full force throughout the country.

The MENTAL HEALTHCARE ACT of 2017 provides for mental healthcare and

services for persons with mental illness. It protects, promotes, and fulfils the rights

of such persons during the delivery of such healthcare and services and for matters

connected in addition to that or incidental thereto.

Definitions

2. (1) In this Act, unless the context otherwise requires,––

(a) "advance directive" means an advance directive made by a person under section

5;

(b) "appropriate Government" means,––

(i) about a mental health establishment established, owned or controlled by the

Central Government or the Administrator of a Union territory having no legislature,

the Central Government;

(ii) about a mental health establishment, other than an establishment referred to in

sub-clause (i), established, owned or controlled within the territory of—

(A) a State, the State Government;

(B) a Union territory having legislature, the Government of that Union territory;

(c) "Authority" means the Central Mental Health Authority or the State Mental Health

Authority, as the case may be;

(d) "Board" means the Mental Health Review Board constituted by the State

Authority under sub-section (1) of section 80 in such manner as may be prescribed;

(e) "caregiver" means a person who resides with a person with mental illness and is

responsible for providing care to that person. And includes a relative or any other

person who performs this function, either free or with remuneration;

(f) "Central Authority" means the Central Mental Health Authority constituted under

section 33;

(g) "clinical psychologist" means a person––

(i) having a recognised qualification in Clinical Psychology from an institution

approved and recognised by the Rehabilitation Council of India, constituted under

section 3 of the Rehabilitation Council of India Act, 1992; or

(ii) having a Post-Graduate degree in Psychology or Clinical Psychology or Applied

Psychology and a Master of Philosophy in Clinical Psychology or Medical and Social

Psychology obtained after completion of a full-time course of two years, which

includes supervised clinical training from any University recognised by the University

Grants Commission established under the University Grants Commission Act, 1956

and approved and recognised by the Rehabilitation Council of India Act, 1992 or

such recognised qualifications as may be prescribed;

(h) "family" means a group of persons related by blood, adoption or marriage;

(i) "Informed consent" means consent given for a specific intervention without any

force, undue influence, fraud, threat, mistake or misrepresentation, and obtained

after disclosing to a person adequate information, including risks and

benefits of,
and alternatives to, the specific intervention in a language and manner understood
by the person; [Practice implication]
(j) "least restrictive alternative", "least restrictive environment", or "less restrictive
option" means offering an option for treatment or a setting for treatment which––
(i) meets the person's treatment needs; and
(ii) imposes the slightest restriction on the person's rights;
(k) "local authority" means a Municipal Corporation or Municipal Council, Zilla
Parishad, Nagar Panchayat, or Panchayat, by whatever name called, and includes
such other authority or body having administrative control over the mental health
establishment or empowered under any law for the time being in force, to function
as a local authority in any city or town or village;
    (l) "Magistrate" means––
(i) about a metropolitan area within the meaning of clause (k) of section 2 of the
Code of Criminal Procedure, 1973, a Metropolitan Magistrate;
(ii) about any other area, the Chief Judicial Magistrate, Subdivisional Judicial
Magistrate or such other Judicial Magistrate of the first class as the State
Government may, by notification, empower to perform the functions of a Magistrate
under this Act;
(m) "medical officer in charge" about any mental health establishment means the
psychiatrist or medical practitioner who, for the time being, is in charge of that mental
health establishment;
(n) "medical practitioner" means a person who possesses a recognised medical
qualification––
(i) as defined in clause (h) of section 2 of the Indian Medical Council Act,

1956, and

whose name has been entered in the State Medical Register, as defined in clause

(k) of that section; or

(ii) as defined in clause (h) of sub-section (1) of section 2 of the Indian Medicine

Central Council Act, 1970, and whose name has been entered in a State Register

of Indian Medicine, as defined in clause (j) of sub-section (1) of that section; or (iii)

as defined in clause (g) of sub-section (1) of section 2 of the Homoeopathy Central

Council Act, 1973, and whose name has been entered in a State Register of Homoeopathy, as defined in clause (i) of sub-section (1) of that section;

(o) "Mental healthcare" includes analysis and diagnosis of a person's mental condition and treatment as well as care and rehabilitation of such person for his

mental illness or suspected mental illness;

(p) "mental health establishment" means any health establishment, including

Ayurveda, Yoga and Naturopathy, Unani, Siddha and Homoeopathy establishment,

by whatever name called, either wholly or partly, meant for the care of persons with

mental illness, established, owned, controlled or maintained by the appropriate

Government, local authority, trust, whether private or public, corporation, cooperative

society, organisation or any other entity or person, where persons with

mental illness are admitted and reside at, or kept in, for care, treatment,

convalescence and rehabilitation, either temporarily or otherwise; and includes any

general hospital or general nursing home established or maintained by the

appropriate Government, local authority, trust, whether private or public,

corporation, co-operative society, organisation or any other entity or

person; but does not include a family residential place where a person with mental illness

resides with his relatives or friends; [Practice implication]

(q) "mental health nurse" means a person with a diploma or degree in general

nursing or a certificate or degree in psychiatric nursing recognised by the Nursing

Council of India established under the Nursing Council of India Act, 1947 and

registered as such with the relevant nursing council in the State;

(r) "mental health professional" means—

(i) a psychiatrist as defined in clause (x); or

(ii) a professional registered with the concerned State Authority under section 55; or

(iii) a professional having a post-graduate degree (Ayurveda) in Mano Vigyan Avum

Manas Roga or a post-graduate degree (Homoeopathy) in Psychiatry or a postgraduate

degree (Unani) in Moalijat (Nafasiyatt) or a post-graduate degree (Siddha) in Sirappu Maruthuvam; [Practice implication]

(s) "mental illness" means a substantial disorder of thinking, mood, perception,

orientation or memory that grossly impairs judgment, behaviour, capacity to

recognise

reality or ability to meet the ordinary demands of life, mental conditions associated

with the abuse of alcohol and drugs, but does not include mental retardation, which

is a condition of arrested or incomplete development of the mind of a person,

specially characterised by sub normality of intelligence; [Practice implication]

(t) "minor" means a person who has not completed the age of eighteen years;

(u) "notification" means a notification published in the Official Gazette, and the

expression "notify" shall be construed accordingly;

(v) "prescribed" means prescribed by rules made under this Act;

(w) "prisoner with mental illness" means a person with mental illness who is an under-trial or convicted of an offence and detained in a jail or prison;

(x) "psychiatric social worker" means a person having a post-graduate degree in

Social Work and a Master of Philosophy in Psychiatric Social Work obtained after

completion of a full-time course of two years, which includes supervised clinical

training from any University recognised by the University Grants Commission

established under the University Grants Commission Act, 1956 or such recognised

qualifications, as may be prescribed; (y) "psychiatrist" means a medical practitioner possessing a post-graduate degree

or diploma in psychiatry awarded by a university recognised by the University Grants

Commission established under the University Grants Commission Act, 1956, or

granted or recognised by the National Board of Examinations and included in the

First Schedule to the Indian Medical Council Act, 1956, or recognised by the Medical

Council of India, constituted under the Indian Medical Council Act, 1956, and

includes, about any State, any medical officer who having regard to his knowledge

and experience in psychiatry, has been declared by the Government of that State

to be a psychiatrist for this Act;

(z) "regulations" means regulations made under this Act;

(za) "relative" means any person related to the person with mental illness by blood,

marriage or adoption;

(ZB) "State Authority" means the State Mental Health Authority established under

section 45.

(2) The words and expressions used and not defined in this Act but defined in the

Indian Medical Council Act, 1956 or the Indian Medicine Central Council

Act, 1970

and not inconsistent with this Act shall have the meanings respectively assigned to

them in those Acts.

Determination of mental illness

3. (1) Mental illness shall be determined in accordance with such nationally or

internationally accepted medical standards (including the latest edition of the Intern

(2) No person or authority shall classify a person as a person with mental illness

except for purposes directly relating to the treatment of the mental illness or in other

matters as covered under this Act or any other law for the time being in force.

(3) Mental illness of a person shall not be determined on the basis of,––

(a) political, economic or social status or membership of a cultural, racial or religious

group, or for any other reason not directly relevant to the mental health status of the

person;

(b) non-conformity with moral, social, cultural, work or political values or religious

beliefs prevailing in a person's community.

(4) Past treatment or hospitalisation in a mental health establishment, though

relevant, shall not by itself justify any present or future determination of the person's

mental illness.

(5) The determination of a person's mental illness shall alone not imply or be taken

to mean that the person is of unsound mind unless he has been declared as such

by a competent court.

Capacity to make mental healthcare and treatment decisions

4. (1) Every person, including a person with mental illness, shall be deemed to have

the capacity to make decisions regarding his mental healthcare or treatment if such

person has the ability to—

(a) understand the information that is relevant to making a decision on the treatment

admission, personal assistance, or

(b) appreciate any reasonably foreseeable consequence of a decision or lack of

decision on the treatment or admission of personal assistance or

(c) communicate the decision under sub-clause (a) by means of speech, expression,

gesture or any other means.

(2) The information referred to in sub-section (1) shall be given to a person using

simple language, which such person understands or in sign language or visual aids

or any other means to enable him to understand the information.

(3) Where a person makes a decision regarding his mental healthcare or treatment

that is perceived by others as inappropriate or wrong, that by itself, shall not mean

that the person does not have the capacity to make mental healthcare or treatment

decision, so long as the person has the capacity to make mental healthcare or

treatment decision under sub-section (1). [Practice implication]

Advance directive

5. (1) Every person who is not a minor shall have a right to make an advance

directive in writing, specifying any or all of the following, namely:––

(a) the way the person wishes to be cared for and treated for a mental illness;

(b) the way the person wishes not to be cared for and treated for a mental illness;

(c) the individual or individuals, in order of precedence, he wants to appoint as his

nominated representative as provided under section 14.

(2) An advance directive under sub-section (1) may be made by a person irrespective of his past mental illness or treatment for the same.

(3) An advance directive made under sub-section (1) shall be invoked only

when

such person ceases to have the capacity to make mental healthcare or treatment

decisions and shall remain effective until such person regains the capacity to make

mental healthcare or treatment decisions.

(4) Any decision made by a person while he has the capacity to make mental

healthcare and treatment decisions shall override any previously written advance

directive by such person.

(5) Any advance directive made contrary to any law for the time being in force shall

be ab initio void.

Manner of making advance directive

6. An advance directive shall be made in the manner as may be specified by the

regulations made by the Central Authority.

Maintenance of online register

7. Subject to the provisions contained in clause (a) of sub-section (1) of section 91,

every Board shall maintain an online register of all advance directives registered

with it and make them available to the concerned mental health professionals as

and when required.

Revocation, amendment or cancellation of advance directive

8. (1) An advance directive made under section 6 may be revoked, amended or

cancelled by the person who made it at any time.

(2) The procedure for revoking, amending or cancelling an advance directive shall

be the same as for making an advance directive under section 6.

Advance directive not to apply to emergency treatment

9. The advance directive shall not apply to the emergency treatment given under

section 103 to a person who made the advance directive.

Duty to follow advance directive

10. It shall be the duty of every medical officer in charge of a mental health establishment and the psychiatrist in charge of a person's treatment to propose or
give treatment to a person with mental illness in accordance with his valid advance
directive, subject to section 11.

Power to review, alter, modify or cancel advance directive
11. (1) Where a mental health professional or a relative or a caregiver of a person
desires not to follow an advance directive while treating a person with mental illness,
such mental health professional or the relative or the caregiver of the person shall
make an application to the concerned Board to review, alter, modify or cancel the
advance directive.
(2) Upon receipt of the application under sub-section (1), the Board shall, after giving
an opportunity of hearing to all concerned parties (including the person whose
advance directive is in question), either uphold, modify, alter or cancel the advance
directive after taking into consideration the following, namely:––
(a) whether the advance directive was made by the person out of his own free will
and free from force, undue influence, coercion, or
(b) whether the person intended the advance directive to apply to the present
circumstances, which may be different from those anticipated or
(c) whether the person was sufficiently well informed to make the decision or
(d) whether the person had the capacity to make decisions relating to his mental
healthcare or treatment when such advanced directive was made or
(e) whether the content of the advance directive is contrary to other laws or
constitutional provisions.
(3) The person writing the advance directive and his nominated

representative shall

have a duty to ensure that the medical officer in charge of a mental health
establishment or a medical practitioner or a mental health professional, as the case

may be, has access to the advance directive when required.

(4) The legal guardian shall have the right to make an advance directive in writing

with respect to a minor, and all the provisions relating to advance directive, mutatis

mutandis, shall apply to such minor till such time he attains majority.

Review of advance directives

12. (1) The Central Authority shall regularly and periodically review the use of

advance directives and make recommendations in respect thereof.

(2) The Central Authority, in its review under sub-section (1), shall give specific

consideration to the procedure for making an advance directive and also examine

whether the existing procedure protects the rights of persons with mental illness.

(3) The Central Authority may modify the procedure for making an advance directive

or make additional regulations regarding the procedure for advance directives to

protect the rights of persons with mental illness.

Liability of medical health professional in relation to advance directive

13. (1) A medical practitioner or a mental health professional shall not be held liable

for any unforeseen consequences of following a valid advance directive.

(2) The medical practitioner or mental health professional shall not be held liable for

not following a valid advance directive if he has not been given a copy of the valid

advance directive.

IMPLICATIONS FOR CLINICAL PRACTICE OF MHA 2017

1. Informed Consent

Since informed consent is given for specific interventions, psychiatrists would need to make sure that informed consent is recorded each time there is a change in

treatment plans. The Act has stipulated that informed consent should be sought

regularly from patients who do not have full capacity (weekly if under Section 89 and

biweekly if under Section 90).

2. Mental Health Establishment

This is the most game-changing definition in the Act, as this has brought under its

scope all health establishments where patients with mental illness reside. With the

exception of a family residence, all other places where a mentally ill person stays

for care are classified as mental health establishments. All these establishments

(residential homes, general hospitals, poor homes, etc.) would require a license to

operate. All admissions and practices would be governed by the Act. This has

enormous implications for human resources, training, governance structures, and

quality of care.

3. Mental Health Professionals

The Act has given significant roles to MHPs. An MHP may admit a voluntary adult

patient without examination or without prior consent from a medical practitioner or

psychiatrist. The MHP would need to be capable of making assessments of mental

illness, its severity, and the benefits of treatments. Furthermore, the MHP must also

be able to assess the patient's capacity to consent to admission and treatment. The

MHP can discharge a voluntary patient. The MHP can also provide independent

recommendations for admission under Sections 89 and 90.

4. Mental Illness The definition covers all mental functioning and thus brings all mental disorders

under its purview. 'Substantial' and 'gross' indicate the seriousness of the mental

illness. The Act covers all admissions, including voluntary admissions, and only

patients who meet this threshold of severity can be admitted. Setting seriousness

criteria for voluntary admissions can be considered as discriminatory to those who

wish to receive treatment for mental disorders that fall short of this threshold. It would

become problematic for a mental health establishment to offer inpatient

interventions (for example, psychological interventions) to patients with mild to

moderate mood, anxiety, and personality disorders, which may not meet the

'substantial' and or 'gross' criteria. The problem is not with the definition of mental

illness but with the setting criteria for voluntary admissions.

5. Capacity Assessment

Capacity assessment would form a key task of admission procedures. For advance

directives and for the appointment of nominated representatives to be valid, the

individual must have the capacity to make these decisions. Section 81 (1) states

that the central authority would appoint an expert committee to issue guidelines for

capacity assessments. If the treating doctor suspects (on reasonable grounds) that

the AD was not made while the person had full capacity and feels that the AD is

preventing appropriate treatment, they should approach the MHRB to change the

AD. Section 13 (1) states that MO cannot be held responsible for the 'unforeseen

'consequences of a valid AD. This implies that the MO must assess the validity of

an AD, especially if the negative consequences are significant. The MHRB can take
up to seven days to decide on appeals to modify AD. Although the Act permits
emergency treatment that contravenes the instructions of a patient's AD, such
treatment is allowed only till the patient is assessed at an MHE. The Act does not
explicitly allow an MHE to deviate from the AD while providing emergency treatment
to patients who are admitted to the MHE.

CHAPTER III

PSYCHIATRIC NURSING IN SCHIZOPHRENIA

General Principles

Nursing care plans and management for schizophrenia involve recognizing schizophrenia, assessing positive and negative symptoms, establishing trust and rapport, reducing symptoms, enhancing communication, maximizing the level of functioning, improving social functioning, developing coping strategies, promoting medication compliance, and evaluating the support system. The essential nursing responsibilities for taking care of patients with schizophrenia can be understood under the following steps.

Step 1: Nursing Assessment (Table 1)

Nursing formulation and daily documentation	A brief formulation of the patient must be documented by the care giving nurse after careful observation of positive, negative, catatonic, cognitive, social interaction problems.
Establish trust and rapport	Empathize, respect person, avoid jokes with patients in the beginning. Hope to build trust and good rapport on a daily basis by individual attention to the patient. Nurse must act as a support to ensure adherence to treatment plan. Always be ethical, respect boundaries.
Assess level of functioning	Nurse must be able to assess the patient's ability to carry out activities of daily living (ADLs) and correlate it with the symptom and treatment response.
Risk assessment	Observe, identify, document for risk to others such as aggression, agitation, command auditory hallucinations, threatening visual hallucinations, delusion of persecution or other delusions towards the care giving team members. Observe, identify, document for risk to self like suicidal thoughts due to command auditory hallucinations, distress from delusions, hallucinations, shame of illness, depression. Early identification of risk is essential for effective management of the same and to avoid use of restraint.
Assess medical status	Monitor vital signs and additional parameters based on medical profile of patient and watch for adverse effects of psychotropic medications and report it to treating psychiatrist.
Assess support system	Talk to patient and understand his/her personal and social circumstances, and identify potential supports in treatment decisions, caregiving, support after discharge, and treatment adherence. Identify expressed emotions, determine disability status.

Table 1: Basic compoenents of Nursing Assessment and Care for Schizophrenia

Step 2: Medical tips

- Impaired Physical Mobility related to depressive mood state and reluctance to initiate movement.
- Impaired social interaction is related to problems in thought patterns and speech.
- Decreased Cardiac Output related to orthostatic hypotensive drug effects.
- Risk for Suicide related to impulsiveness and marked changes in behaviour.
- Risk for Injury related to hallucinations and delusions.
- Risk for Imbalanced Nutrition: less than body requirements related to self-neglect and refusal of self-care.

Nursing Care Planning and Goals
- Reduce the severity of psychotic symptoms
- Prevent recurrence of acute episodes
- Meet the patient's physical and psychosocial needs
- Help patient gain optimum level of functioning
- Increase patient's compliance to treatment and nursing plan

Nursing Interventions

• **Establish trust and rapport.** Please don't touch the patient without telling him first what you will do. Use an accepting, consistent approach; short, repeated contacts are best until trust has been established. Language should be unambiguous. Maintain a sense of hope for possible improvement and convey this to the patient.

• **Maximize level of functioning.** Avoid promoting dependence by doing only what the patient can't do for himself. Reward positive behaviour and work with him to increase his sense of responsibility in improving functioning.

• **Promote social skills.** Provide support in assisting him to learn social skills.

• **Ensure safety.** Maintain a safe environment with minimal stimulation.

• **Ensure adequate nutrition.** Monitor the patient's nutritional status, and if the patient thinks his food is poisoned, let him fix his food if possible or offer him foods in closed containers that he can open. Institute suicide and/ or homicide precautions as appropriate.

• **Keep it accurate.** Engage patients in reality-oriented activities that involve human contact (e.g., workshops, inpatient social skills training). Clarify private language, autistic inventions, or neologisms.

• **Deal with hallucinations by presenting reality**. Explore the content of hallucinations. Avoid arguing about the hallucinations. Tell them you do not see, hear, smell, or feel it, but explain that you know that these hallucinations are real to him.

• **Promote compliance and monitor drug therapy**. Administer prescribed drugs and encourage the patient to comply. Ensure that patient is really taking the drug. Observe for manifestations that warrant hypersensitivity reactions and toxicity.

• **Encourage family involvement**. Involve family in patient treatment and teach members to recognize impending relapse (e.g. nervousness, insomnia, decreased ability to concentrate). Suggest ways how families can manage symptoms.

Evaluation

• Evaluate effectiveness of drug therapy (absence of acute episodes and psychotic symptoms).

• Evaluate compliance to health instructions (taking medications on time, showing independence in activities, involvement of family).

• Level of patient's functioning (ability to engage in social interactions).

• Patient's mental status (oriented to reality).

Documentation Guidelines

The following are to be documented in the patient's chart:

• Document the assessed presenting signs and symptoms (e.g., positive and negative signs).

• In instituting suicide precaution, document behaviour and your precautions.

• In instituting homicide precaution, document patient's comment and who was notified. Be sure to notify the doctor and the potential victim.

• In using restraints, document time of application and release.

Nursing Problem Priorities

The following are the nursing priorities for patients with schizophrenia:

• Establish therapeutic rapport and trust

• Monitor and manage symptoms

• Administer antipsychotic medications

• Provide education and support

• Assist with daily living skills

• Collaborate with interdisciplinary team

• Ensure a safe environment

Nursing Assessment

Assess for the following subjective and objective data:
• Positive symptoms of schizophrenia:
• Delusions – Persistent false beliefs
• Hallucinations – Sensory experiences without external stimuli
• Disorganized thinking – Incoherent or illogical thought processes
• Abnormal motor behaviour – Unusual or unpredictable movements
• Negative symptoms of schizophrenia:
• Reduced emotional expression – Diminished display of emotions
• Social withdrawal – Decreased interest in social interactions
• Lack of motivation – Decreased drive or initiative
• Impaired cognition – Difficulties with attention, memory, and problem-solving

Nursing Diagnosis

Following a thorough assessment, a nursing diagnosis is formulated to specifically address the challenges associated with schizophrenia based on the nurse's clinical judgment and understanding of the patient's unique health condition. While nursing diagnoses serve as a framework for organizing care, their usefulness may vary in different clinical situations. In real-life clinical settings, it is important to note that the use of specific nursing diagnostic labels may not be as prominent or commonly utilized as other
components of the care plan. It is ultimately the nurse's clinical expertise and judgment that shape the care plan to meet the unique needs of each patient, prioritizing their health concerns and priorities.

Nursing Goals

Goals and expected outcomes may include:
• The patient will express thoughts and feelings in a coherent, logical, goal directed manner.
• The patient will demonstrate reality-based thought processes in verbal communication.
• The patient will spend time with one or two other people on structured activity neutral topics.
• The patient will spend two to three five-minute sessions with the nurse sharing observations in the environment within three days.
• The patient will be able to communicate in a manner that can be understood by others with the help of medication and attentive listening by the time of discharge.

• The patient will learn one or two diversionary tactics that work for him/her to decrease anxiety, hence improving the ability to think clearly and speak more logically.

• The patient will maintain interaction with another patient while doing an activity (e.g., a simple board game, or drawing).

• The patient will demonstrate interest to start coping skills training when ready for learning.

• The patient will engage in one or two activities with minimal encouragement from the nurse or family members.

• The patient will state that he or she is comfortable in at least three structured activities that are goal-directed.

• The patient will learn ways to refrain from responding to hallucinations.

• The patient will state that the voices are no longer threatening, nor do they interfere with his or her life.

• The patient will state, using a scale from 1 to 10, that "the voices" are less frequent and threatening when aided by medication and nursing intervention.

• The patient will identify personal interventions that decrease or lower the intensity or frequency of hallucinations (e.g., listening to music, wearing headphones, reading out loud, jogging, and socializing).

• The patient will demonstrate techniques that help distract him or her from the voices.

• The patient remains free from injury as evidenced by the absence of wounds and abrasions.

• The patient will develop trust in at least one staff member within one week. The patient will sustain attention and concentration to complete tasks or activities.

• The patient will state that the "thoughts" are less intense and less frequent with the help of medications and nursing interventions.

• The patient will talk about concrete happenings in the environment without talking about delusions for five minutes.

• The patient will demonstrate two effective coping skills that minimize delusional thoughts.

• The patient will be free from delusions or demonstrate the ability to function without responding to persistent delusional thoughts.

• The patient will demonstrate learn the ability to remove himself or herself from situations when anxiety begins to increase with the aid of medications and nursing interventions.

• The patient will demonstrate decreased suspicious behaviours regarding interaction with others.

• The patient will be able to apply a variety of stress/anxiety-reducing techniques on their own.

• The patient will acknowledge that medications will lower suspiciousness.

• The patient will state that he/she feels safe and more in control with interactions with the environment/family/work/social gatherings.

• The family and/or significant others will recount in some detail the early signs and symptoms of relapse in their ill family member, and know whom to contact in case.

• The family and/or significant others will state and have written information identifying the signs of potential relapse and whom to contact before discharge.

• The family and/or significant others will state that they have received needed support from community and agency resources that offer education, support, coping skills training, and/or social network development (psychoeducational approach).

• The family and/or significant others will state what medications can do for their ill family member, the side effects and toxic effects of the drugs, and the need for adherence to medication at least 2 to 3 days before discharge.

• The family and/or significant others will name and have a complete list of community supports for ill family members and supports for all members of the family at least 2 days before the discharge.

• The family and/or significant others will attend at least one family support group (single family, multiple families) within 4 days from the onset of the acute episode.

• The family and/or significant others will meet with the nurse/physician/ social worker on the first day of hospitalization and begin to learn about neurologic/biochemical disease, treatment, and community resources.

• The family and/or significant others will problem-solve, with the nurse, two concrete situations within the family that all would like to discharge. The family and/or significant others will recount in some detail the early signs and symptoms of relapse in their ill family member, and know whom to contact.

• The family and/or significant others will demonstrate problem-solving skills for handling tensions and misunderstandings among the family member.

• The family and/or significant others will have access to family/multiple family support groups and psycho-educational training.

Nursing Interventions and Actions

Therapeutic interventions and nursing actions for patients with schizophrenia may include:

1. Promoting Patient Safety

Patients with schizophrenia are prone to injury due to auditory and visual hallucinations caused by abnormalities in the brain's processing of sensory information. These hallucinations can be distressing and interfere with the patient's ability to function in daily life. These patients may have difficulty distinguishing between reality and their hallucinations, leading to further confusion and disorientation. Patients diagnosed with schizophrenia also have a risk of substance abuse and violence, which can also result in injuries to the patient or to others around them.

Be alert for signs of increasing fear, anxiety, or agitation.

This might herald hallucinatory activity, which can be very frightening to the patient, and the patient might act upon command hallucinations (harm self or others). A few patients may act violently as a result of command hallucinations or delusions, or the violence may be associated with substance abuse. These violent acts are often highly publicized, and the intense publicity has the unfortunate consequence of exacerbating the stigma of the disease.

Explore how the patient experiences the hallucinations.

Exploring the hallucinations and sharing the experience can help give the person a sense of power that he or she might be able to manage the commanding, hallucinatory voices. One of the paradoxical features of self in schizophrenia is that the I is neither fully oneself nor another but an in-between state between pure observation (passivity) and participation; the patient might experience a vicious circle in which phases of psychosis feed into and reinforce each other.

Assess for the potential of substance abuse.

Alcohol and drug abuse are common in schizophrenia for reasons that are not entirely clear. For some people, these drugs provide relief from symptoms of the illness or the adverse effects of antipsychotic medications, and the drive for this relief is strong enough to allow even patients who are impoverished and disorganized to find substances to abuse.

Observe for obsessive-compulsive symptoms.

Several patients with schizophrenia display obsessive-compulsive symptoms, such as the need to check, count, or repeat certain activities.

Obsessive-compulsive symptoms are a known adverse effect of some antipsychotic medications, particularly clozapine.

Help the patient to identify the needs that might underlie the hallucination. What other ways can these needs be met?

Hallucinations might reflect needs for anger, power, self-esteem, and sexuality. Patients diagnosed with schizophrenia revealed in a study that sometimes, when they have a problem that is a burden on their minds, they tend to want to tell their problems to family members. However, they are afraid to tell their family members because they feel that when they tell them their problems, their family members will also be burdened by the problem. Thus, patients choose to keep their problems to themselves.

Accept that the voices are accurate to the patient, but explain that you do not hear the voices. Refer to the voices as "your voices" or "voices you hear".

Validating that your reality does not include voices can help the patient cast "doubt" on the validity of his or her voice. Do not argue with the hallucinations or deluded observations of the patient. Instead, explain to the patient that you have your perceptions of the world; do not focus on correcting their negative thoughts or encouraging their distorted reality.

Help the patient identify times when the hallucinations are most prevalent and frightening.

This helps both nurse and patient identify situations and times that might be most anxiety-producing and threatening to the patient. Complications occur when the hallucinations command the patient to hurt themselves or others. The paracusia, perceived as coming through the ears, on the surface of the body, in the mind, or anywhere in an external space, can also be so self-deprecating that it causes the patient to attempt suicide.

• If voices tell the patient to harm themself or others, take necessary environmental precautions.

• Notify others, including police, physicians, and administration, according to unit protocol.

• If in the hospital, use unit protocols for suicide or threats of violence if the patient plans to act on commands.

• If in the community, evaluate the need for hospitalization.

In many cases, swift, decisive intervention can prevent a person from committing suicide or harming others. Because of this preventable aspect of suicide, recognizing and taking action if the potential arises is critical. Based on the clinical assessment and all of the information available, if the person is indeed suicidal or homicidal, the intervention should consist of multiple steps.

Document what the patient says, and if he/she is a threat to others, document who was contacted and notified (use agency protocol as a guide).

People often obey hallucinatory commands to kill themselves or others. Early assessment and intervention might save lives. A clear and complete evaluation and clinical interview provide the information upon which to base a suicide intervention.

Suicidal ideation is highly linked to completed suicide. If suicidal ideation is present, the next question must be about any plans for suicidal acts.

Stay with patients when they are starting to hallucinate and direct them to tell the "voices they hear" to go away. Repeat often in a matter-of-fact manner.

The patient can sometimes learn to push voices aside when given repeated instructions, especially within the framework of a trusting relationship. The individual must not be left alone. In the emergency department, such a recommendation is handled easily by hospital security personnel. In other settings, summon assistance quickly. Involve family or friends; they can remain with the patient while treatment arrangements are made.

Decrease environmental stimuli when possible (low noise, minimal activity).

This decreases the potential for anxiety that might trigger hallucinations and helps calm the patient. Stress and anxiety can trigger or worsen hallucinations, delusions, and other symptoms, leading to increased distress and impaired functioning. Creating a calm environment can reduce sensory overload, providing a stable and predictable atmosphere to help patients manage their symptoms more effectively.

Intervene with one-on-one, seclusion, or PRN medication (As ordered) when appropriate.

Intervene before anxiety begins to escalate. If the patient is already out of control, use chemical or physical restraints following unit protocols. The suicidal patient should be treated initially in a secure, safe, and highly supervised place. Inpatient care at a hospital offers one of the best settings. Most managed care companies recognize the medical necessity of hospitalization in situations in which the suicide danger is acute.

Keep to simple, essential, reality-based topics of conversation. Help the patient focus on one idea at a time.

The patient's thinking might be confused and disorganized; this intervention helps the patient focus and comprehend reality-based issues. The patient may also show thought blocking, in which long pauses occur before they answer a question. The patient has little insight into their problems; therefore, reinforcing reality is necessary. Work with the patient to find which activities help reduce anxiety and distract the patient from hallucinatory material. Practice new skills with the patient. If patients' stress triggers hallucinatory activity, they might be more motivated to find ways to remove themselves from a stressful environment or try distraction techniques. Engaging the patient in vocational and art therapy can improve self-esteem and help integrate their functioning.

Engage the patient in reality-based activities such as card playing, writing, drawing, doing simple arts and crafts, or listening to music.

Redirecting the patient's energies to acceptable activities can decrease the possibility of acting on hallucinations and help distract from voices. The nurse should remember that the activity has to be within the patient's functioning level. Some activities are drawing, reading, listening to music, or walking. These are activities in the "here and now". Keeping the patient focused on reality-based activities is vital in helping them cope with these symptoms.

Arrange referrals for a dual-diagnosis treatment program for a patient with substance abuse.

Patients who abuse substances may fare better in dual-diagnosis treatment programs, in which principles from the mental health field can be integrated with principles from the chemical dependency field.

Remove all dangerous objects in the patient's room. Remove anything that the patient may use to hurt or kill themselves. Remove sharp or potentially hazardous objects. Ask the patient for any weapon, such as knives or pills, and secure them away from the patient. Removal of ligature points (places where things

like ropes could be attached) is associated with significant reductions in the overall psychiatric inpatient suicide rate and the rate of inpatient suicide by hanging.

Prepare the patient for cognitive behavioural therapy (CBT).

A study of brief CBT in a cohort of active-duty military personnel who either attempted suicide or experienced suicidal ideation found the treatment effective in preventing follow-up suicide attempts. Data showed that soldiers treated with brief CBT were approximately 60% less likely to attempt suicide than soldiers who did not receive the therapy.

2. Establishing Therapeutic Relationships and Promoting Therapeutic Communication

Establishing a therapeutic relationship and promoting communication with patients with schizophrenia involves creating a safe and non-judgmental environment where the individual feels comfortable expressing themselves. Active listening, empathy, and validating their experiences can foster trust and encourage open communication. Using clear and simple language, providing visual aids if necessary, and allowing ample time for the patient to process information can enhance understanding and facilitate effective communication.

Assess if incoherence in speech is chronic or if it is more sudden, as in an exacerbation of symptoms.

Establishing a baseline facilitates the establishment of realistic goals, the foundation for planning effective care. In measuring disorganized speech, communication impairment focuses on the communication failures in speech, rather than the underlying thought disorder. Communication impairment can be assessed very sensitively and reliably and has been found to be elevated in first-degree relatives of people with schizophrenia.

Identify the duration of the psychotic medication of the patient.

Therapeutic levels of an antipsychotic aid clear thinking and diminishes derailment or looseness of association. The patient may be calmer and less agitated almost immediately during the beginning of antipsychotic medications, but the alleviation of the psychosis itself takes several weeks.

Measure the extent of the patient's communication impairment by the Communication Disturbances Index (CDI).

One conceptualization of disorganized speech is communication impairment, which refers to frequent instances of significant speech unclarity and is typically measured by the CDI. The CDI rates speech based on the occurrence of language that fails to communicate the intended message through unclear references or grammatical disturbances.

Look for themes in what is said, even though spoken words appear incoherent (e.g., fear, sadness, guilt).

Often the patient's choice of words is symbolic of feelings. The patient's speech may be difficult to follow because of the looseness of his or her associations; the sequence of thoughts follows a logic that is clear to the patient but not to the interviewer. The speech may be circumstantial (the patient takes a long time and uses many words in answering a question) or tangential (the patient speaks at length but never actually answers the question).

Keep the voice in a low manner and speak slowly as much as possible.

A high-pitched/loud tone of voice can elevate anxiety levels while slow speaking aids understanding. Emotions are subjective feelings about an event. The way the person communicates and relates with others is influenced by his or her emotional state. Emotions such as sadness, anxiety, anger, and fear affect health workers' communication with others.

Keep the environment calm, quiet, and as free of stimuli as possible.

A calm environment helps keep anxiety from escalating and increasing confusion and hallucinations/delusions. Stress and anxiety can trigger or worsen hallucinations, delusions, and other symptoms, leading to increased distress and impaired functioning.

Creating a calm environment can reduce sensory overload, providing a stable and predictable atmosphere.

Plan short, frequent periods with a patient throughout the day.

Short periods are less stressful, and periodic meetings give a patient a chance to develop familiarity and safety. Patients with schizophrenia may struggle with organization and planning. A structured, short period of activity can help the patient manage their daily activities and self-care routines.

Use clear or simple words, and keep directions simple as well.

The patient might have difficulty processing even simple sentences. The patient may show thought blocking, in which long pauses occur before he or she answers a question.

The patient's thoughts may also be disorganized, stereotyped, or perseverative.

Use simple, concrete, and literal explanations.

Minimizes misunderstanding and/or incorporates those misunderstandings into delusional systems. The patient also has difficulty with abstract thinking, demonstrated by the inability to understand common proverbs or idiosyncratic interpretations of them.

Focus on and direct the patient's attention to concrete things in the environment. This helps draw focus away from delusions and focus on reality-based things. Don not focus on correcting their psychotic thinking or encourage their distorted reality.

Emphasize that you are there as a support and can get help if need be. Reinforce reality by expressing that each has its own perceptions of the world.

When you do not understand a patient, let him/her know you are having difficulty understanding.

Pretending to understand limits your credibility in the eyes of your patient and lessens the potential for trust. Do not argue with the hallucinations or deluded observations. It is not useful to challenge the person who is struggling. Instead, refrain from being judgemental and work to stay engaged with the patient.

When the patient is ready, introduce strategies that can minimize anxiety and lower voices, and "worrying" thoughts, and teach the patient to do the following:

• Focus on meaningful activities.

• Learn to replace negative thoughts with constructive thoughts.

• Learn to replace irrational thoughts with rational statements.

• Perform deep breathing exercises.

• Read aloud to self.

• Seek support from staff, family, or other supportive people.

• Use a calming visualization or listen to music.

Helping the patient to use tactics to lower anxiety can help enhance functional speech. People with schizophrenia will experience cognitive, emotional, perceptual, and behavioural disturbances. Distortion of negative thoughts that appear in schizophrenic patients can trigger mental stress, resulting in anxiety, depression, or even an urge to commit suicide. This is a consequence that must be avoided at all costs.

Use therapeutic techniques (clarifying feelings when speech and thoughts are disorganized) to try to understand the patient's concerns. Even if the words are hard to understand, try getting to the feelings behind them. Therapeutic communication is consciously planned communication, aims, and activities centered on the patient's recovery. In this relationship, the patient feels valued, accepted, and directed. Patients will voluntarily express their feelings and thoughts so that the emotional burden and tension they feel can disappear entirely and return to normal.

Establish rapport and build a trusting relationship with the patient.

Trust is needed to build effective communication between nurses and patients. This variable occurs in the implementation of therapeutic communication at each phase. The trust built from the start creates a sense of comfort and creates a therapeutic environment. Building a trusting relationship will make the relationship smoother going forward because the patient and the nurse are more open about the problems they face.

Provide positive feedback and appreciation to the patient.

Praise given to patients when they do something positive is considered more valuable. With sincere appreciation, patients will feel valued and cared for. Giving appreciation is a form of reward for patients. This can be done during the work and termination phases of the nurse-patient relationship.

Assess if the medication has reached therapeutic levels.

Many of the positive symptoms of schizophrenia (hallucinations, delusions, racing thoughts) will subside with medications, which will facilitate interactions. Study data showed that the long-acting injectable (LAI) antipsychotic formulation of risperidone proved superior to oral risperidone on measures of relapse and symptom control. It also provided better control of hallucinations and delusions.

Identify with the patient the symptoms he experiences when he or she begins to feel anxious around others.

Increased anxiety can intensify agitation, aggressiveness, and suspiciousness. Many patients with schizophrenia report symptoms of anxiety. It is unclear whether such anxiety is an independent problem, part of schizophrenia, a reaction to schizophrenia, or a complication of treatment. Anxiety may precede the onset of schizophrenia for several years.

Keep the patient in an environment as free of stimuli (loud noises, crowding) as possible.

The patient might respond to noises and crowding with agitation, anxiety, and an increased inability to concentrate on outside events. A calm environment can be an essential component of treatment for patients with schizophrenia. It can help reduce stress and anxiety, provide a sense of safety and security, and provide structure and routine, all of which can help the patient manage their symptoms more effectively and lead to better outcomes.

Avoid touching the patient.

Touch by an unknown person can be misinterpreted as a sexual or threatening gesture. This is particularly true for a paranoid patient. It appears that some social processing systems are intact or largely intact in schizophrenia, whereas others are clearly impaired. For example, social cue recognition, the ability to process a diverse array of social cues from faces, voices, and body movements, is impaired in schizophrenia. Ensure that the goals set are realistic; whether in the hospital or community. This avoids pressure on the patient and a sense of failure on the part of the nurse/ family. This sense of failure can lead to a mutual withdrawal. If goals are set too high or unrealistic, the patient may become frustrated and discouraged, leading to decreased motivation and engagement in treatment. Achieving goals, even small ones, can help the patient feel a sense of accomplishment and increase their confidence and motivation.

Structure activities that work at the patient's pace and activity.

The patient can lose interest in activities that are too ambitious, which can increase a sense of failure. Motivation refers to what people are willing to do and includes the direction, intensity, and persistence of goal-directed behaviour. Structure times each day to include planned times for brief interactions and

activities with the patient on a one-on-one basis This helps the patient to develop a sense of safety in a non-threatening environment. The problems of social motivation in schizophrenia can stem from disturbances in either type of motivational drive. For example, those with prominent clinically rated asociality show diminished social approach motivation and a lack of motivation to seek out social

interactions. However, others show elevated social avoidance in that they are interested in social connections but do not attempt to engage due to fear of rejection.

If the patient is unable to respond verbally or in a coherent manner, spend frequent, short periods with patients. An interested presence can provide a sense of being worthwhile. Patients with schizophrenia may experience social isolation due to the stigma associated with the disorder or the symptoms they experience. The quiet presence of the nurse can provide a social connection for patients, helping them feel less alone.

If the patient is found to be very paranoid, solitary or one-on-one activities that require concentration are appropriate.

The patient is free to choose his level of interaction; however, concentration can help minimize distressing paranoid thoughts or voices. Most patients with schizophrenia may act violently as a result of command hallucinations or delusions. Engaging in short periods of cognitive activity, such as playing a game, reading a book, or doing a puzzle, can help improve cognitive function and enhance overall mental health.

If the patient is delusional/hallucinating or is having trouble concentrating at this time, provide very simple concrete activities with the patient (e.g., looking at a picture or doing a painting).

Even simple activities help draw patients away from delusional thinking into reality in the environment. Art therapy activities such as colouring or drawing can help the patient improve their concentration and reduce stress. Encourage them to choose a simple colouring book or sketch pad and focus on the colours and shapes as they create.

If the patient is very withdrawn, one-on-one activities with a "safe" person initially should be planned.

Learn to feel safe with one person, then gradually might participate in a structured group activity. Many patients with schizophrenia report symptoms of depression. It is unclear whether such depression is an independent problem, part of schizophrenia, a reaction to schizophrenia, or a complication of treatment. Addressing this issue is important because of the high rate of suicide among these patients.

Try to incorporate the strengths and interests the patient had when not as impaired into the activities planned.

This increases the likelihood of the patient's participation and enjoyment. By focusing on the things that the patient enjoys and is good at, the nurse can help them feel more motivated and engaged in their treatment. This can increase their overall satisfaction with the therapy and may lead to better outcomes. Teach the patient to remove himself briefly when feeling agitated and work on some anxiety relief exercises (e.g., meditations, rhythmic exercise, deep breathing exercise).

Teach the patient skills in dealing with anxiety and increasing a sense of control.

Techniques such as deep breathing, mindfulness, and progressive muscle relaxation can help patients calm down and feel more in control. Encouraging the patient to practice these techniques regularly can help them build skills for managing their agitation. Useful coping skills that the patient will need include conversational and assertiveness skills. These are fundamental skills for dealing with the world, which everyone uses daily with more or less skill. Problem-solving with constructive coping is problem-solving in a positive way. Nurses teach this to the patients to build an understanding of their problems so that they can solve them in a positive way. Remember to give acknowledgment and recognition for positive steps the patient takes in increasing social skills and appropriate interactions with others.

Recognition and appreciation go a long way to sustaining and increasing a specific behaviour. Provide appreciation by praising the patient when they do something positive.

This will be more valuable to the patient than appreciation in the form of goods. This way, the patient will feel more valued and cared for.

Provide opportunities for the patient to learn adaptive social skills in a nonthreatening environment. Initial social skills training could include basic social behaviours (e.g., appropriate distance, maintaining good eye contact, calm manner/behaviour, moderate voice tone).

Social skills training helps the patient adapt and function at a higher level in society and increases the patient's quality of life. Abilities linked to social processes referred to as social cognition include such processes as perceiving social cues, sharing other people's experiences, and inferring other people's thoughts and emotions. Social cognition tends to have stronger associations with a social disability, suggesting that social cognitive abilities are building blocks for interpersonal interactions and productive activities.

As the patient progresses, provide the patient with graded activities according to the level of tolerance e.g., (1) simple games with one "safe" person; (2) slowly add a third person into "safe".

Gradually the patient learns to feel safe and competent with increased social demands. Socialization group activity therapy is an effort to facilitate the socialization skills of a number of patients with social relationship problems, which aims to improve social relations within a group gradually, where patients can introduce themselves, are able to get acquainted with group members, are able to converse with group members, and are able to convey and discuss conversational topics.

As the patient progresses, coping skills training should be available to him/her (nurse, staff, or others). Basically, the process:

• Define the skill to be learned.
• Model the skill.
• Rehearse skills in a safe environment, then in the community.
• Give corrective feedback on the implementation of skills.

This increases the patient's ability to derive social support and decreases loneliness. Patients will not give up the substance of abuse unless they have alternative means to facilitate socialization they belong. Studies have concluded that coping skills training is effective in improving mental and physical health and mitigating behavioural and social problems. Another study showed that coping skills training increased self-esteem and improved group interaction, while it led to a decrease in depression and isolation. Eventually engage other patients and significant others in social interactions and activities with the patient (card games, ping pong, sing-a-songs, group sharing activities) at the patient's level.

The patient continues to feel safe and competent in a graduated hierarchy of interactions. Schizophrenia affects the person's whole family, and the family's responses can affect the trajectory of the person's illness. Some studies have found that family therapy or family interventions may prevent relapse, reduce hospital admission, and improve medication adherence.

Prepare the patient for cognitive remediation.

Cognitive remediation is a treatment modality derived from principles of neuropsychological rehabilitation and is based, in part, on the idea that the brain has some plasticity and that brain exercises can encourage neurons to grow. Cognitive remediation works best when patients are stable. Improvement occurs across numerous cognitive functions.

Refer the patient to vocational rehabilitation.

Most patients with schizophrenia would like to work; employment can improve income, self-esteem, and social status. Supported employment programs currently thought to be most effective are those that offer individualized, supported, and rapid job assignments and that is integrated with other services. These programs are associated with higher rates of employment.

3. Improving Thought Organization and Reality Orientation

Helping patients with thought organization involves assisting them in organizing their thoughts, encouraging logical thinking, and addressing any disorganized thought processes. Reality orientation involves gently reminding patients of the current time, place, and situation, and helping the patient differentiate between what is real and what may be distorted or influenced by their illness, thereby promoting a clearer perception of reality.

Identify feelings related to delusions. For example:

• If a patient believes someone is going to harm him/her, the patient is experiencing fear.

• If a patient believes someone or something is controlling his/her thoughts, the patient is experiencing helplessness.

When people believe that they are understood, anxiety might lessen. Asking if the patient is hearing voices can be an early intervention. If the patient is experiencing hallucinations, this must be reported immediately.

Hallucinations, delusions, and paranoia are scary for them. Understanding and patience are the most important characteristics of caring for this patient.

Attempt to understand the significance of these beliefs to the patient at the time of their presentation.

Important clues to underlying fears and issues can be found in the patient's seemingly illogical fantasies. According to a study, thoughts and other internal mental processes turn inwards as objects of observation. Patients can experience a sense of not being in control of one's mental processes. As one continues this introspective process, willingly or not, thoughts become increasingly alien and detached from the very self that is supposed to protect the integrity of thinking.

Recognize the patient's delusions as the patient's perception of the environment.

Recognizing the patient's perception can help you understand the feelings he or she is experiencing. Do not pretend to see or hear the patient's hallucinations. Likewise, do not agree with the delusions or paranoia. Do not try to convince the patient that what they are experiencing is not real. To them it is real. State that "I know the voices are real to you, but I do not hear them" to allow the nurse to be honest and help the patient accept that the voices are not real. This allows the patient to gain control over the thoughts.

Assess attention span and distractibility. Note the level of anxiety.

Attention span and ability to attend or concentrate may be severely shortened, which both causes and potentiates anxiety, affecting thought processes. The patient may become agitated or anxious. Offer empathy such as "You seem anxious. How can I help you?" this offers validation of the patient's feelings and reinforces trust.

Explain the procedures and try to be sure the patient understands the procedures before carrying them out.

When the patient has full knowledge of procedures, he or she is less likely to feel tricked by the staff. It is important to remember that patients with schizophrenia can have difficulty with memory. Repeating steps or phrases several times may be required.

Interact with patients on the basis of things in the environment. Try to distract patients from their delusions by engaging in reality-based activities (e.g., card games, simple arts and crafts projects, etc).

When thinking is focused on reality-based activities, the patient is free of delusional thinking during that time. This helps focus attention externally. When a patient experiences delusions, it is important to focus on reality. Activities should be one-on-one for a suspicious patient some activities to consider are drawing, reading, or walking.

Keeping the patient focused on reality-based activities is important in helping them cope with their symptoms. Do not touch the patient; use gestures carefully. Suspicious patients might misinterpret touch as either aggressive or sexual in nature and might interpret it as a threatening gesture. People who are psychotic need a lot of personal space. Nonverbal communication involves what is not said but rather involves tone of voice, stance, eye contact, facial expressions, and movements. When interacting

with the patient be sure to face the person, maintain eye contact, stand near the person but not too close, and try to position at the patient's level, facial expression should show your interest or concern, and speak slowly and calmly.

Initially do not argue with the patient's beliefs or try to convince the patient that the delusions are false and unreal.

Arguing will only increase the patient's defensive position, thereby reinforcing false beliefs. This will result in the patient feeling even more isolated and misunderstood. It is okay to ask about the delusion to obtain assessment information, however, do not argue or deny the belief. The patient may be using delusions as an attempt to understand their environment.

• Encourage healthy habits to optimize functioning:
• Maintain medication regimen.
• Maintain regular sleep patterns.
• Maintain self-care.
• Reduce alcohol and drug intake.

All are vital in helping keep the patient in remission. Adherence is usually overestimated by both the patient and the healthcare provider. Nonadherence can be partial or complete, but even partial adherence is associated with relapse. Many psychotropic medications can cause weight gain and changes in glucose or lipid metabolism. Therefore, the patient should be encouraged to be as physically active as possible.

Show empathy regarding the patient's feelings; reassure the patient of your presence and acceptance.

The patient's delusion can be distressing. Empathy conveys your caring, interest, and acceptance of the patient. Notice that the responsibility of understanding the patient is placed on the nurses or caregivers. This helps the patient understand how they are being perceived and alleviates any anxiety or blame for the patient.

Teach the patient coping skills that minimize "worrying" thoughts. Coping skills include:
• Going to a gym
• Phoning a helpline
• Singing or listening to a song.
• Talking to a trusted friend

When the patient is ready, teach strategies the patient can do alone. Coping strategies capture a variety of trait-dependent activities approached to deal with challenges driven by stressful experiences. It has been reported that patients with schizophrenia tend to prefer avoidance coping over adaptive coping. A lower preference for active coping strategies and a preference for dysfunctional coping has also been associated with greater severity of positive and depressive symptoms as well as cognitive impairment.

Utilize safety measures to protect patients or others, if the patient believes they need to protect themselves against a specific person. Precautions are needed. During the acute phase, patients' delusional thinking might dictate to them that they might have to hurt others or themselves in order to be safe. External controls might be needed. The nurse should first take measures to protect themselves. When interacting

with the patient, make sure that the door is closer to not between the nurse and the patient. A clear escape route should be accessible if needed. The nurse should call for help if needed and never try to handle the situation themselves.

Maintain consistency in staff assigned to the patient to the extent possible. This provides the patient with feelings of stability, familiarity, and control of the situation. If the patient is suspicious, attempt to promote trust by using the same staff if possible and being honest with the patient.

Arrange for referrals to cognitive remediation therapy.

Cognitive remediation creates improvements across numerous cognitive functions, and changes are found in brain imaging that reflect these changes in brain functioning.

Cognitive remediation techniques are time-intensive and labor-intensive. Because cognitive deficits are multiple and vary from person to person, such techniques seem to work best when specifically tailored to each patient.

Promote smoking cessation.

Most patients with schizophrenia smoke. This may be a result of previous conventional antipsychotic treatment, in that nicotine may ameliorate some of the adverse effects of these drugs. Smoking may also be related to the boredom associated with hospitalizations, the peer pressure from other patients to smoke, or the anomie associated with unemployment.

4. Promoting Effective Coping Strategies

Coping strategies for patients with schizophrenia involve developing adaptive ways to manage symptoms and daily challenges. These may include engaging in stress-reducing activities such as exercise, practicing relaxation techniques, participating in supportive therapy or support groups, maintaining a structured routine, and utilizing problem-solving skills to address specific difficulties. Developing a strong support network of family, friends, and mental health professionals can also provide valuable emotional and

practical support in coping with the impact of schizophrenia.

Assess and observe patients regularly for signs of increasing anxiety and hostility.

Intervene before the patient loses control. Persons with schizophrenia may display strange and poorly understood behaviours. These include drinking water to the point of intoxication, staring at themselves in the mirror, performing stereotyped activities, hoarding useless objects, and mutilating themselves. Their wake-sleep cycle may also be disturbed, further predisposing the patient to anxiety and the development of hostility.

Asses for causes or predisposing factors of the agitation or violence.

Individuals with schizophrenia and a positive history of adverse childhood experiences (ACEs) tend to show higher levels of psychotic symptoms, greater cognitive deficits, worse response to antipsychotic treatment, and greater functional impairment. The Childhood Experience of Care and Abuse Questionnaire (CECA-Q) is used to collect data on exposure to ACEs. Additionally, substance abuse may be associated with violence in patients with schizophrenia.

Note expressions of indecision, dependence on others, and the inability to manage own activities of daily living.

This may indicate the need to lean on others for a time. Early recognition and intervention can help the patient regain equilibrium. A lower preference for active coping strategies and a preference for dysfunctional coping have been associated with greater severity of positive and depressive symptoms as well as cognitive impairment, making the patient more dependent upon others.

Assess the presence of positive coping skills and inner strengths. When the patient has coping skills that have been successful in the past, they may be used in the current situation to relieve tension and preserve the patient's sense of control. However, limitations of the condition may impact the choices available to the

patient, such as listening to rock music is not recommended for patients experiencing auditory hallucinations.

Explain to the patient what you are going to do before you do it.

This prepares the patient beforehand and minimizes misinterpreting their intent as hostile or aggressive. Patients diagnosed with schizophrenia due to adverse childhood experiences may be more prone to experience subsequent adversities through increased stress sensitivity and threat anticipation.

Use a nonjudgemental, respectful, and neutral approach with the patient.

There is less chance for a suspicious patient to misinterpret intent or meaning if the content is neutral and the approach is respectful and non-judgemental. Stating "I know that the voices are real to you, I do not hear them" allows the nurse to be honest and may help the patient accept that the voices are not real. This allows the patient to gain control of hallucinations and delusions.

Use clear and simple language when communicating with a suspicious patient. This minimizes the opportunity for miscommunication and misconstruing the meaning of the message. The patient may also exhibit concrete or literal thinking. Avoid using abstract phrases or cliches such as "the early bird gets the worm". This can be misinterpreted by the patient. Clarify what the patient is stating by asking, "I am not sure what you mean or I am not sure what you are trying to tell me. Can you try to explain it to me again please?".

Diffuse angry verbal attacks with a non-defensive stand. When staff becomes defensive, anger escalates for both the patient and staff. A nondefensive and non-judgemental attitude provides an atmosphere in which feelings can be explored more easily. When interacting with the patient, be sure to face the patient,

maintain eye contact, stand near the patient but not too close so they can still have their personal space, try to position at the patient's level, facial expressions should show interest or concern, and speak slowly and calmly. Set limits in a clear matter-of-fact way, using a calm tone. "Giving threatening remarks is unacceptable. We can talk more about the proper ways in dealing with your feelings". A calm and neutral approach may diffuse the escalation of anger. Offer an alternative to verbal abuse by finding appropriate ways to deal with feelings. When these behaviours cause problems, it is important to develop reasonable rules and to set consequences for breaking those rules. This process is called setting limits. It can be helpful to all people

involved because it sets out clearly what is acceptable and what is not. The type of limits set would depend on the patient's situation. Be honest and consistent with the patient regarding expectations and enforcing

rules. Suspicious people are quick to discern honesty. Honesty and consistency provide an atmosphere in which trust can grow. In order for the rules to work, the nurse must make sure that they are willing to follow through on consequences. The patient should clearly understand the rules and the consequences.

Maintain a low level of stimuli and enhance a non-threatening environment (avoid groups). Noisy environments might be perceived as threatening. Knowing what to expect from the patient and what triggers the symptoms is important to care for the patient. The nurse should also recognize if the patient is agitated, anxious, or stressed. Furthermore, it is important to know what can be done to help alleviate the patient's discomfort.

Be aware of the patient's tendency to have ideas of reference; do not do things in front of the patient that can be misinterpreted, such as laughing or whispering and talking quietly when the patient can see but not hear what is being said. Suspicious patients will automatically think that they are the target of the interaction and interpret it in a negative manner (e.g., you are laughing or whispering about them).

Furthermore, be aware that the patient may believe that their food is poisoned or controlled. Offer food that they can open themselves with supervision or allow them to choose between actions so they feel some control over their environment.

Initially, provide solitary, non-competitive activities that take some concentration. Later a game with one or more patients that takes concentration (e.g., chess checkers, thoughtful card games such as ridge or rummy). If a patient is suspicious of others, solitary activities are the best. Concentrating on environmental stimuli minimizes paranoid rumination.

Results of a study indicate that there is an effect of Socialization Group Activity Therapy on the socialization ability of respondents before and after the intervention. Problems in interacting with other people stemmed from the absence of action or stimulus that can change maladaptive behaviour patterns and a less therapeutic environment.

Provide verbal/physical limits when the patient's hostile behaviour escalates: "We cannot allow you to verbally attack someone here. If you can't hold/control yourself, we are here in order to help you".

Often verbal limits are effective in helping a patient gain self-control. If help is needed, the nurse should call for one and never attempt to handle the situation alone. The door should be closer to not between the nurse and the patient and a clear escape route should be there if needed. The nurse should always be aware of the surroundings and understand how to recognize agitation or anxiety in the patient.

Encourage family members or parents to provide emotional support.

There is an important role of parental support that enhances the development of more adaptive coping strategies. Early parental loss may exceed the individual cognitive capacity to understand and cope with this experience as well as it may disrupt the further development of coping strategies. Adults who experienced early parental loss have been shown to report more substance use, behavioural disengagement, and emotional eating.

Establish a therapeutic nurse-patient relationship.

The patient may feel less inhibited in the context of this relationship to verbalize feelings of helplessness and powerlessness and feel more freedom to discuss changes that may be necessary for the patient's life to improve the situation. Trust is needed to build effective communication, and the trust built from the start creates a sense of comfort and a therapeutic environment.

5. Initiating Patient Education and Health Teachings

Patient education and health teachings for patients with schizophrenia involve providing information about the illness, its symptoms, and treatment options, as well as teaching coping skills, medication management, and stress reduction techniques. By empowering patients with knowledge and practical strategies, they can actively participate in their own care, make informed decisions, and improve their ability to manage their condition effectively.

Assess the family member's current level of knowledge about the disease and medications used to treat the disease.

Family might have misconceptions and misinformation about schizophrenia and treatment or no knowledge at all. Teach the patient's and family's level of understanding and readiness to learn. Lack of knowledge about mental illness has been described as one of the components of the stigma construct itself. Poorer knowledge about mental illness has been linked to stigmatizing attitudes in several studies.

Identify the family's ability to cope (e.g., the experience of loss, caregiver burden, needed support).

The family's needs must be addressed to stabilize the family unit. Family burden in schizophrenia has certain established domains, of which family relations and social interactions are important. Objective burdens of care reflect the tangible aspects of caregiving, such as financial issues, while subjective burdens reflect how caregivers perceive and evaluate their situations in relation to an illness.

Assess role expectations of family members and encourage discussion about them.

Each person may see the situation in their own individual manner, and clear identification and sharing of these expectations promote understanding. Role theory considers the unmet expectations of caregivers from an ill person as a major cause of their mental burdens. Individuals have their own roles within a family and are expected to fulfil these roles. However, schizophrenia often makes it difficult to satisfy these expectations, which has a negative impact on family relationships.

Note cultural and religious beliefs.

These affect the patient and family members' reaction and adjustment to the diagnosis, treatment, and outcomes. According to a study, the majority of caregivers were female, in keeping with the commonly observed preponderance of women in caregiving roles in India. Overall, female caregivers seemed to be more closely involved in the care of the patient with schizophrenia, and were sometimes the only ones left in the family who were still in contact with the patient. Male caregivers, on the other hand, appeared generally more distant to the patient, and possibly less isolated through stigma.

Inform the patient's family in clear, simple terms about psychopharmacologic

therapy: dose, duration, indication, side effects, and toxic effects. Written information should be given to the patient and family members as well.

Understanding the disease and the treatment of the disease encourages greater family support and patient adherence. The nature of schizophrenia makes it a potentially difficult illness for patients and family members to understand. Nevertheless, teaching

them to understand the importance of medication adherence and of abstinence from alcohol and other drugs of abuse is important.

Teach the patient and family the warning symptoms of relapse.

Rapid recognition of early warning symptoms can help ward off potential relapse when immediate medical attention is sought. It is helpful to work with the patient so that both patient and family can learn to recognize early signs of decompensation such as insomnia or increased irritability. Education may improve adherence to medication and may help the patient and family members cope with the illness better in other ways. Provide information on disease and treatment strategies at the family's level of understanding.

This meets family members' needs for information. Because other illnesses are common in schizophrenia, education about the importance of a healthy lifestyle and regular healthcare is helpful. Counselling with respect to sexuality, pregnancy, and sexually transmitted diseases is important for these patients and their families too.

Provide an opportunity for the family to discuss feelings related to an ill family member and identify their immediate concerns.

Nurses and staff can best intervene when they understand the family's experience and needs. Most caregivers reported in a study a great emotional burden as the result of the patient's condition. Caregivers' reported emotions were dominated by an emphasis on worry and tension. Furthermore, caregivers expressed feelings of frustration and anger toward the patient, often triggered by having to look after them with very little support. In addition, some revealed feelings of shame associated with the patient's appearance or behaviour in public, or simply having a mentally ill family member. Provide information on patient and family community resources for the patient and family after discharge: day hospitals, support groups, organizations, psychoeducational programs, community respite centers (small homes), etc. These

groups can provide education and support. Groups, support groups, and psychoeducational centers can help:

• Access caring

• Access resources

- Access support

Develop family skills
- Improve the quality of life for all family members
- Minimizes isolation

Listen for expressions of helplessness and hopelessness.
The joy of the recovery of the patient is often quickly replaced by grief and anger at the "loss" of the pre-diseased person and the necessity of dealing with the new person that the family does not know and may not even like. Prolongation of these feelings may result in depression.

Provide information about the family intervention.
Family intervention has been established as an evidence-based practice to reduce relapse and rehospitalization in patients with this disorder (Shiraishi & Reilly, 2018). Familial "high expressed emotion" (hostile overinvolvement and intrusiveness) leads to more frequent relapses. Some studies found that family therapy or family interventions may also improve medication adherence.

Identify and encourage the use of previously successful coping behaviours. Most people have developed effective coping skills that can be useful in dealing with the current situation. Health services for patients with schizophrenia need to create spaces where caregivers can speak openly about their own experiences of stigma and other needs. Respite help, contact with peer support groups, and opportunities to access

healthcare, and emotional, and social support in their own right should be facilitated for caregivers where feasible and appropriate.

6. **Administer Medications and Provide Pharmacologic Support**
Schizophrenia medications include typical antipsychotics and atypical antipsychotics. These medications work by modulating dopamine and serotonin receptors to manage positive and negative symptoms of schizophrenia, and the choice of medication depends on individual factors and symptom severity. Clozapine, a unique atypical antipsychotic, may be used for treatment-resistant cases, and additional medications like mood stabilizers and benzodiazepines may be prescribed to address specific symptoms or

comorbidities.

Typical Antipsychotics:
1. **Chlorpromazine:** This medication helps to alleviate symptoms of

psychosis by blocking dopamine receptors in the brain. It can help reduce hallucinations and delusions but may also cause side effects such as sedation and movement disorders.

2. Haloperidol: Another dopamine receptor antagonist, haloperidol is known for its effectiveness in treating positive symptoms of schizophrenia. It has a lower risk of sedation compared to some other antipsychotics but may have a higher potential for movement-related side effects.

3. Fluphenazine: Like other typical antipsychotics, fluphenazine blocks dopamine receptors. It can be administered orally or by injection and may have side effects such as sedation, movement disorders, and sexual dysfunction.

Atypical Antipsychotics

1. **Risperidone:** This medication targets both dopamine and serotonin receptors, making it effective in treating positive and negative symptoms of schizophrenia. Risperidone is available in both oral and long-acting injection forms.

2. **Olanzapine:** Olanzapine also acts on dopamine and serotonin receptors and effectively manages both positive and negative symptoms. It is available in oral and injection formulations and may be associated with weight gain and metabolic side effects.

3. **Quetiapine:** Quetiapine is primarily a dopamine and serotonin receptor antagonist, used for both positive and negative symptoms of schizophrenia. It is generally well-tolerated but can cause sedation and weight gain.

4. **Aripiprazole:** Aripiprazole functions as a partial dopamine agonist, balancing dopamine activity in the brain. It effectively manages positive symptoms and may lower the risk of movement-related side effects.

5. **Ziprasidone:** Ziprasidone targets dopamine and serotonin receptors, reducing positive and negative symptoms. It may have a lower risk of weight gain but can cause changes in heart rhythm.

6. **Clozapine:** Clozapine is sometimes recommended for the treatment of patients with schizophrenia who are violent. It is the oldest atypical antipsychotic agent and probably the most effective. Approximately one-third of patients who have not responded to conventional antipsychotic agents do better on clozapine. Violence, hostility, and suicidality may be diminished with the use of clozapine.

Mood stabilizers (e.g., lithium carbonate, valproate): These medications are sometimes used in conjunction with antipsychotics to manage mood symptoms and stabilize mood fluctuations in individuals with schizophrenia.

CHAPTER IV

PSYCHIATRIC NURSING IN BIPOLAR DISORDER

What are Bipolar Disorders?

Bipolar disorders, which in the ICD-10 is classified as bipolar disorder, or manicdepressive illness (MDI), is a common, severe, and persistent mental illness. This condition is a serious lifelong struggle and challenge. In the 5th edition of the Diagnostic and Statistical Manual of Mental Disorders (DSM-5), bipolar disorder constitutes a spectrum of mood disorders that includes BP-I, BP-II, and cyclothymia, and is thought to
be a "bridge" between schizophrenia spectrum disorders and depressive disorders in terms of the symptomatology, family history, and genetics.

The diagnosis of bipolar disorder type I (BP-I) requires the presence of a manic episode of at least one week's duration or that leads to hospitalization or other significant impairment in occupational or social functioning. The episode of mania cannot be caused by another medical illness or by substance abuse. These criteria are based on the specifications of the DSM-5.

According to DSM-5, the general diagnostic criteria for bipolar and related disorders include the following:

• **BD-I:** Criteria met at least for one manic, which might have been preceded or followed by a hypomanic episode or major depressive episode.

• **BD-II:** Criteria met for at least one current or past hypomanic episode and a major depressive episode. There should be no manic episodes.

• **Cyclothymic disorder:** Hypomania symptoms that do not meet the criteria for hypomanic episodes and depressive symptoms that do not meet the criteria for major depressive episodes in numerous periods for at least two years. The criteria for major depressive, manic, or hypomanic episodes should never have been met.

• **Specified bipolar and related disorders:** Bipolar-like phenomena that do not meet criteria for BD-I, BD-II, or cyclothymic disorder due to insufficient duration or severity.

• **Unspecified bipolar and related disorders:** Characteristic symptoms of bipolar and related disorders that cause clinically significant distress or impairment in social, occupational, or other important areas of functioning but do not meet the full criteria for any category previously mentioned.

Nursing Care Plans and Management

Nursing care planning goals for patients with bipolar disorder include: providing a safe environment, improving self-esteem, enhancing social support, encouraging selfcare independence, guiding patients toward socially appropriate behaviour, promoting family involvement, and providing education about the condition and how to manage it effectively.

Nursing Problem Priorities

The following are the nursing priorities for patients with bipolar disorders:

• Mood stabilization. Managing and stabilizing mood fluctuations to minimize the severity and duration of manic and depressive episodes in patients with bipolar disorder.

• Medication adherence. Ensuring consistent adherence to prescribed medications to effectively manage symptoms and prevent relapses.

• Suicide risk assessment and prevention. Assessing and monitoring the risk of suicide in patients with bipolar disorder, implementing appropriate interventions, and providing support to prevent self-harm.

• Psychoeducation and self-management skills. Providing education to patients and their families about bipolar disorder, its symptoms, triggers, and strategies for managing the condition to enhance self-awareness and empower them to actively participate in their treatment.

• Psychosocial support and therapy. Offering psychosocial support, counselling, and therapy to address emotional challenges, improve coping skills, and enhance overall quality of life for patients with bipolar disorder.

Nursing Assessment

Assess for the following subjective and objective data:

Nursing Diagnosis

Following a thorough assessment, a nursing diagnosis is formulated to specifically address the challenges associated with bipolar disorders based on the nurse's clinical judgment and understanding of the patient's unique health condition. While nursing diagnoses serve as a framework for organizing care, their usefulness may vary in different clinical situations. In real-life clinical settings, it is important to note that the use of specific nursing diagnostic labels may not be as prominent or commonly utilized as other

components of the care plan. It is ultimately the nurse's clinical expertise and judgment that shape the care plan to meet the unique needs of each patient, prioritizing their health concerns and priorities.

Nursing Goals

Goals and expected outcomes may include:

• The patient will respond to the medication within the therapeutic levels.

• The patient will sustain optimum health through medication management and a therapeutic regimen.

• The patient will drink 8 oz of fluid every hour throughout the day while in the acutely manic stage.

• The patient will remain free from falls and abrasions every day while in the hospital.

• The patient will be free of dangerous levels of hyperactive motor behaviour with the aid of medications and nursing interventions within the first 24 hours.

• The patient will spend time with the nurse in a quiet environment three to four times a day between 7 AM and 11 PM with the aid of nursing guidance.

• The patient will take short voluntary rest periods during the day.

• The patient will be free of excessive physical agitation and purposeless motor activity within two weeks.

• The patient will be free of injury within two to three weeks:

• Stable cardiac status.

• Skin free of abrasions and scrapes.

• Well-dehydrated.

• The patient will verbalize control of feelings.

• The patient will respond to external controls (medications, seclusion, nursing interventions) when potential or actual loss of control occurs.

• The patient will refrain from provoking others to physical harm, with the aid of seclusion or nursing interventions.

• The patient will display nonviolent behaviour toward others in the hospital, with the aid of medications and nursing interventions.

• The patient will seek help when experiencing aggressive impulses.

• The patient will refrain from verbal threats and loud, profane language toward others.

• The patient will be safe and free from injury.

• The patient will initiate and maintain goal-directed and mutually satisfying activities/verbal exchanges with others.

• The patient will find one or two solitary activities that can help relieve tensions and minimize the escalation of anxiety with the aid of a nurse or occupational/activity therapist.

• The patient will focus on one activity requiring a short attention span of 5

minutes three times a day with nursing assistance.
• The patient will sit through a short, small group meeting free from disruptive outbursts.
• The patient will demonstrate an ability to remove themself from a stimulating environment in order to "cool down" by discharge. The patient will participate in unit activities without disruption or demonstrating inappropriate behaviour by discharge.
• The patient will put feelings into words instead of actions when experiencing anxiety or losing control before discharge.
• The patient will report an absence of delusions, racing thoughts, and irresponsible actions as a result of medication adherence and environmental structures.
• The patient will return to the pre-crisis level of functioning after the acute/severe manic phase is past.
• The patient will cease the use of manipulation to obtain needs and control others.
• The patient will demonstrate an absence of destructive behaviour toward self or others.
• The patient will be protected from making any major life decisions (legal, business, marital) during an acute or severe manic phase.
• The patient will respond to limit-setting techniques with aid of medication during the acute and severe manic phases.
• The patient will respond to external controls (medication, seclusion, nursing intervention) when potential or actual loss of control occurs.
• The patient will retain valuables or other possessions while in the hospital.
• The patient will demonstrate a decrease in manipulative behaviour.
• The patient will demonstrate a decrease in demanding and provocative behaviour.
• The patient will seek competent medical assistance and legal protection when signing any legal documents regarding personal or financial matters during the manic phase of illness.
• The family members and/or significant others will discuss with the nurse/counsellor three areas of family life that are most disruptive and seek alternative options with aid of nursing/counselling interventions.
• The family members and/or significant others will state and have in writing the names and telephone numbers of at least two bipolar support groups.
• The family members and/or significant others will state that they have

gained support from at least one support group on how to work with family members when he or she is manic.

• The family members and/or significant others will state their understanding of the need for medication adherence, and be able to identify three signs that indicate a possible need for intervention when their family member's mood escalates.

• The family members and/or significant others will briefly discuss and have in writing, the names and addresses of two bipolar organizations, two Internet site addresses, and medication information regarding bipolar disorder. The family members and/or significant others will state that they find needed

support and information in a support group (s).

• The family members and/or significant others will identify the signs of increased manic behaviour in their family members. The family members and/or significant others will state what they will do (whom to call, where to go) when the patient's mood begins to escalate to dangerous levels.

• The family members and/or significant others will demonstrate an understanding of what bipolar disorder is, the medications, and the need for adherence to medication and treatment.

• The patient will sleep six hours out of 24 with aid of medication and nursing measures within three days.

• The patient will eat half to one-third of each meal plus one snack between meals with aid of nursing intervention.

• The patient will have normal bowel movements within 2 days with the aid of high-fiber foods, fluids, and if needed, medication.

• The patient will wear appropriate attire each day while in the hospital.

• The patient will bathe at least every other day while in the hospital.

• The patient will sleep six to eight hours per night.

• The patient will have a weight within normal limits for age and height.

• The patient will have bowel habits within normal limits.

• The patient will dress and groom themself in an appropriate manner consistent with the pre-crisis level of dress and grooming.

Nursing Interventions and Actions

Therapeutic interventions and nursing actions for patients with bipolar disorders may include:

1. Promoting Safety and Preventing Injury

Patients with bipolar disorder are at risk for injury due to a combination of affective, cognitive, and psychomotor factors that can affect their judgment, impulsivity, and coordination. Furthermore, bipolar disorder is associated with neurologic imbalances, which can further increase the risk of injury. Exhaustion, dehydration, and rage may also contribute to the risk of injury in patients with bipolar disorder. The main complications of bipolar disorder, or manic-depressive illness (MDI) are suicide, homicide, and addictions. Patients with bipolar disorder may also experience neurologic imbalances that can contribute to the development of manic episodes, psychotic symptomatology, and rage. During manic episodes, patients may engage in impulsive and reckless behaviour, including aggression and violence toward themselves or others.

Additionally, the presence of psychotic symptoms and rage can further increase the risk of violent behaviour in individuals with bipolar disorder. Aggressive behaviour in bipolar disorder shows a direct prognostic value, being linked to suicide attempts and more frequent hospitalizations, the severity of mania, the presence of mixed symptoms, and comorbid borderline personality disorder.

Assess the patient's current mood and behaviour, observe for signs of a manic or depressive episode, as well as any impulsive or reckless behaviour that may increase the risk of injury. This is to determine whether the patient is currently experiencing a manic, depressive, or stable state. This information will identify potential risks for injury and take measures to prevent harm to the patient or others. Patients emerging from depression are thought to be at an increased risk of suicide. The risk of self-destructive behaviour and death is lifelong.

Assess the patient's cognitive function, including attention, memory, and decisionmaking skills.

The patient's cognitive function will identify any deficits or impairments that may increase

their risk of injury. Symptoms of mania may include reckless behaviour without regard for

consequences and severe thought disturbances. Patients in the manic phase can become

homicidal by acting on delusions.

Assess the patient's use of substances, including alcohol and drugs. Some substances can worsen the symptoms of bipolar disorder or trigger mood episodes such as depression or mania. Substance use can also lead to further complications and increase the risk of harm, including accidents, injuries, or even overdose. One major area of concern is the relationship between violent crime and bipolar disorder. This danger is particularly present and prominent with patients who have a substance abuse problem.

Observe for signs of lithium toxicity (e.g., nausea, vomiting, diarrhoea, drowsiness, muscle weakness, tremor, lack of coordination, blurred vision, or ringing in the ears). There is a small margin of safety between therapeutic and toxic doses. Symptoms of intoxication include coarse tremors, hyperreflexia, nystagmus, and ataxia. Patients often show varying levels of consciousness, ranging from mild confusion to delirium.

Gastrointestinal effects typically occur within one hour of ingestion.

Observe the patient for indications for inpatient management.

Patients diagnosed with bipolar mania or depression and severe symptoms must be referred for urgent/emergent mental health intervention. The indications for inpatient treatment in a person with bipolar disorder, include the danger to self, danger to others, delirium, marked psychotic symptoms, total inability to function, total loss of control, and medical conditions that warrant medication monitoring.

Provide structured solitary activities with the assistance of a nurse or aide.

The structure provides focus and security. Patients with bipolar disorder are especially sensitive to the disruption of routines. A malfunctioning body clock is a prime suspect in the causes of the dramatic mood shifts that define the bipolar disorder, according to research published in Current Psychiatry Reports. A routine also allows the patient to feel some sense of control in their life.

Provide frequent rest periods.

This prevents exhaustion. Sleep deprivation may be associated with poor eating habits in bipolar patients, given the association of sleep deprivation with certain hormonally influenced responses that lead to enhanced caloric intake.

Furthermore, sleep disturbances in bipolar disorder are linked to reduced energy levels and thus, a lessened likelihood of engaging in other healthy behaviours. Encourage the patient to communicate openly about their feelings and concerns, and provide a nonjudgmental and supportive environment.

This can help the patient develop coping strategies and problem-solving skills to manage their symptoms and minimizes the risk of impulsive or risky behaviours. Patients with bipolar disorder may need to take medications and attend therapy sessions to manage their condition. Open communication helps patients feel more comfortable talking to their

healthcare providers about their symptoms and any concerns they may have about their treatment. Open communication can help identify triggers and warning signs of mood episodes. This helps them take action early to prevent or lessen the severity of mood
episodes.

Maintain a low level of stimuli in the patient's environment (e.g., loud noises, bright
light, low-temperature ventilation). This helps minimize the escalation of anxiety. A highly-stimulating environment can trigger symptoms of mania or hypomania in patients with bipolar disorder. Overstimulation, such as loud noise, bright lights, or a fast-paced environment, can disrupt sleep patterns,
increase irritability and anxiety, and trigger racing thoughts and impulsive behaviour.

Encourage the patient to engage in activities that are safe and structured, such as
exercise or creative activities. Exercise has been shown to have mood-stabilizing effects and can help minimize the severity and frequency of mood swings in patients with bipolar disorder. Patients in the
depressed phase are encouraged to exercise. These individuals should try to develop a regular daily schedule of major activities, especially times of going to bed and waking up. A regular exercise schedule should be proposed for all patients, especially those with bipolar disorder. Both exercise and a regular schedule are keys to surviving this illness. Provide a safe and supportive environment for the patient, including ensuring that the patient's room is free from potential hazards and that safety measures are in place (such as bed rails or padded walls).

Patients with bipolar disorder may experience symptoms that can impair their judgment, increase impulsivity, and heighten the risk of accidents or self-harm. Therefore, it is essential to reduce potential hazards in the patient's environment and provide safety measures as needed. Homicidal patients, often in the manic phase, can be very demanding and grandiose. In this context, they are angered if others do not immediately comply with their wishes, and they can turn dramatically violent. Administer phenothiazines for acute mania and enforce seclusions to decrease any physical harm.
Exhaustion and death result from dehydration, lack of sleep, and constant physical activity. Phenothiazine antipsychotics, which are classified as first-

generation antipsychotics, are efficacious for treating both psychotic and non-psychotic manic and mixed episodes, as well as hypomania.

Redirect violent behaviour.

Physical exercise can decrease tension and provide focus. If the patient diagnosed with bipolar disorder does not have strategies to cope with irritability, it can lead to angry outbursts. Many patients with bipolar disorder experience anger, which can appear out of character for them.

Protect the patient from giving away money and possessions. Hold valuables in a hospital safe until rational judgment returns.

The patient's "generosity" is a manic defense that is consistent with irrational, grandiose thinking. In some cases, extreme grandiosity can take the form of delusions or fixed beliefs unsupported by facts and reality. For example, the patient may run through their savings buying expensive gifts for loved ones because they feel convinced that they are about to get a promotion and significant raise.

Work with the patient to develop a safety plan that includes methods to manage mood swings and prevent injury, as well as emergency contacts and resources.

The safety plan can help patients recognize when they are at risk for injury and take steps to prevent it. It also ensures a rapid response in case of a crisis. Therefore, preventing harm to the patient and others. Patients with a possible diagnosis of bipolar depression must also be referred for urgent/emergent mental health intervention if they present with serious delusion, visual/auditory hallucinations, confusion, catatonic behaviour, extreme negativism/mutism, and/or inappropriate affect of a bizarre or odd quality. Assist in transferring the patient to the appropriate facility or with the admission process.

The treatment of bipolar disorder is directly related to the phase of the episode and the severity of that phase. For example, a person who is extremely depressed and exhibits suicidal behaviour requires inpatient treatment. If the patient is in a short-term inpatient care unit and has not made significant progress, reevaluate the management strategy. Transfer to a long-term inpatient care unit might also be considered.

Place the patient in suicide precautions.

A patient with bipolar disorder, especially one in a depressive episode, may present with a significant risk for suicide, especially those with an early onset of symptoms. Serious suicide attempts and specific ideation with plans to constitute clear evidence of the need for constant observation and preventive protection; consider referring these individuals to mental health specialty care. A sign on the door indicating visitors need to report to the nurse's station prior to entering the room. All sharp objects and unnecessary cables, cords, shoe laces, and equipment should be removed from the patient's room.

Linens should be limited. A designated suicide watcher may be appointed as appropriate. Frequently assess the patient's behaviour for signs of increased agitation and hyperactivity.

Early detection and intervention of escalating mania will prevent the possibility of harm to self or others, and decrease the need for seclusions. Sometimes, a patient's behaviour can be totally out of control, which is a particular concern during a manic episode. In this situation, the patient's behaviours are so beyond limits that they destroy their career and can be harmful to those around them.

Assess for predictors of aggressive and violent behaviour. There is consensus amongst researchers that there is a positive association between underlying mental disorders, such as bipolar disorder, and violent behaviour. According to the NICE Expert Committee Report, a lifetime prevalence of violence in the non-psychiatric population of 7.3% was lower than those with underlying mental illness at 16.1%. The
tendency towards violent behaviour increases in the presence of substance misuse, irrespective of the presence of underlying mental disorders.

Perform a mental status examination.
A mental state examination should be attempted before sedating the patient. This often proves difficult to accomplish in the context of a violent and aggressive patient; however, healthcare professionals should document their attempt at accomplishing this task including the findings. The goal is to uncover the underlying aetiology of the patient's aggressive and violent behaviour.

Use a calm and firm approach.
This provides structure and control for a patient who is out of control. Remain calm, maintain a confident and competent demeanour, and attempt to de-escalate by engaging the patient in a conversation.

Use short, simple, and brief explanations or statements.
A short attention span limits the understanding of small pieces of information. Simple sentences are easier to understand, especially for patients who may be experiencing agitation. Clear communication can reduce misunderstandings and potential triggers for aggressive behaviour.

Remain neutral as possible; do not argue with the patient.

The patient can use inconsistencies and value judgments as justification for arguing and escalating mania. Avoid arguments between staff members in front of the patient too. Use brief sentences to maintain control of the conversation and prevent the patient from becoming more agitated or escalating the situation.

Maintain a consistent approach, employ consistent expectations, and provide a structured environment.

Clear and consistent limits and expectations minimize the potential for patients' manipulation of staff. Limit-setting helps establish clear boundaries for acceptable behaviour. By setting limits, patients understand what is expected of them and what is not tolerated, which can reduce the likelihood of aggressive behaviour in the future. Redirect agitation and potentially violent behaviours with physical outlets in an area of low stimulation (e.g., punching bag). This can help to relieve pent-up hostility and relieve muscle tension. Providing the patient with safe choices can help give them a sense of control and reduce feelings of frustration and powerlessness. If the patient is fixated on a particular issue or behaviour, it can help to redirect their attention to something else.

Decrease environmental stimuli (e.g., by providing a calming environment or assigning a private room)

This helps decrease the escalation of anxiety and manic symptoms. It is important to find a balance between stimulation and calmness for patients with bipolar disorder. The patient should still have access to social and physical activities to promote positive mental health, but the environment should also provide adequate opportunities for rest, relaxation, and downtime.

Alert staff if a potential for seclusion appears imminent. The usual priority of interventions would be: firmly setting limits, chemical restraints (tranquilizers), and seclusions. If nursing interventions (quiet environment and firm limit setting) and chemical restraints (tranquilizers–e.g., haloperidol [Haldol]) have not helped dampen escalating manic behaviours, then seclusion might be warranted. Non-antipsychotic medication approaches for agitation are discussed first, followed by a review of the relevant antipsychotics.

Chart, in nurse's notes, behaviours; interventions; what seemed to escalate agitation; what helped to calm agitation; when as-needed (PRN) medications were given and their effect; and what proved most helpful.

Staff will begin to recognize potential signals for escalating manic behaviours and have a guideline for what might work best for the individual patient. Differentiating patterns of violence central to the development of a differential diagnosis is achieved by analysing the pattern of the violence. Whether aggressive episodes are singular or repetitive, with low or high potential for the actual injury, helps guide the clinician in formulating immediate treatment management plans and a long-term strategy. Ensure plans or protocols are in place in case of an incident with an aggressive or violent patient. Staff, especially those working in emergency departments, should prepare, anticipate, and readily prevent aggression. Every health facility must have laid down protocols to ensure the safety of all patients and staff. The protocol should contain the triage plan for early signs of aggression and the roles of each staff in such a situation. There must also be backup plans for the safety of staff, patients, and properties, such as placing security personnel and acquiring services from the local police department, and the emergency medical personnel. Each healthcare facility must have a designated place/room for calming down aggressive and violent patients and regular monitoring.

Administer pharmacologic agents as indicated.

The aim is to reach calm within a maximum period of two hours whilst avoiding adverse effects. Olanzapine was the most frequently studied drug in a systemic review. Changes at two hours showed the strongest effect for haloperidol plus promethazine, risperidone, olanzapine, droperidol, and aripiprazole. Adverse effects are most prominent for haloperidol and haloperidol plus lorazepam. Oral benzodiazepines should be prioritized, according to the Essential Drug List, because it is the safest route.

Consider using restraints carefully and in line with protocols and the patient's rights.

Manual restraints may be necessary to administer treatment to the patient. Mechanical restraints should be used only when absolutely necessary to protect the patient and others in an acute setting for as short a period as possible. Types, sites, and duration of any restraints used must be documented with 15-minute monitoring of vital signs, the mental state, restraint sites, and reasons for use.

2. Providing Therapeutic Communication

Patients with bipolar disorder may experience impaired social interaction due to their mood swings, which can make it difficult to maintain stable relationships and communicate effectively. Additionally, the high levels of energy and agitation that are associated with bipolar disorder can make it difficult for patients to focus and engage in social situations. Finally, the stigma surrounding mental illness may also contribute to social isolation and difficulties in forming relationships for individuals with bipolar disorder.

Assess the patient's current mood state and level of agitation or hyperactivity. During manic episodes, individuals with bipolar disorder may experience heightened energy levels, impulsivity, and agitation, which can affect the ability to engage in social interactions in a healthy and productive way. The mood disturbance during a manic episode is sufficient to cause impairment at work or danger to the patient or others. The mood is not the result of substance abuse or a medical condition.

Assess the patient's communication abilities and ability to interpret social cues. During manic episodes, persons with bipolar disorder may talk excessively or incoherently, making it difficult for others to understand. While during depressive episodes, individuals may experience social withdrawal and can become unresponsive, or have difficulty expressing thoughts and feelings. In both cases, these communication barriers can affect the individual's ability to engage in social interactions and form meaningful relationships with others.

Explore any past experiences with social relationships and determine any underlying factors that may be contributing to the patient's difficulties with social interaction, such as anxiety or previous traumas.

These factors can guide effective management strategies and help address the origin of the patient's social difficulties. Poorer symptomatic profiles have previously been associated with lower levels of social support, a greater number of future mood episodes, and more severe self-reported depressive symptoms. A critical and hostile family atmosphere significantly predicts the rate of relapse into acute mood episodes.

Assess the patient's psychosocial functioning.

A study suggested that the assessment of psychosocial functioning should involve different to live independently, and to engage in romantic life, with functional recovery typically being defined as the restoration of normal role functioning in the domains under scrutiny.

Common assessment tools that can be used include the Global Assessment Functioning Scale (GAF), the Functioning Assessment Short Test (FAST) scale, and the WHO Organization Disability Assessment Schedule 2.0 (WHODAS 2.0). These tools are core set specific for bipolar disorder.

When less manic, the patient might join one or two other patients in quiet, nonstimulating activities (e.g., drawing, board games, cards).

As mania subsides, involvement in activities that provide a focus and social contact becomes more appropriate. Competitive games can stimulate aggression and can increase psychomotor activity. Non-stimulating activities can also help reduce stress, anxiety, and agitation, which are common symptoms of bipolar disorder. Other nonstimulating activities may include reading, taking a walk, meditating, and painting. When possible, provide an environment with minimum stimuli (e.g., quiet, soft music, dim lighting).

Reduction in stimuli lessens distractibility. Patients diagnosed with bipolar disorder may experience an increase in energy and excitement in response to stimulating environments or activities. However, an increase in energy can also trigger manic or hypomanic episodes. An environment with minimum stimuli can help reduce the risk of triggering these episodes.

Solitary activities requiring short attention spans with mild physical exertion are best initially (e.g., writing, taking photos, painting, or walks with staff).

Solitary activities minimize stimuli; mild physical activities release tension constructively. These activities can also help promote relaxation, improve mood, and provide a sense of purpose and accomplishment. However, it is important to note that while these activities can be helpful for managing symptoms of bipolar disorder, they should not be used as a substitute for professional treatment.

Encourage the patient to engage in social activities, such as joining a support group or attending community events.

Social isolation is a common problem for people with bipolar disorder, which can aggravate symptoms and make it harder to maintain relationships. Studies have examined the positive effects of social experiences on bipolar disorder, such as social support. Providing information regarding specific characteristics that could facilitate better mood management. For example, when other people listened to and understood their bipolarrelated experiences, or how reassurance from a friend changed negative thought processes.

Provide information to the patient and family on bipolar disorder and its impact on social interaction.

Educating the patients and families about the symptoms, causes, and treatments of bipolar disorder enables a good understanding of the condition. This will minimize the stigma and misconceptions surrounding the disorder, which can in turn improve communication and relationships between patients and their loved ones. Previous research has documented that caregivers perceived bipolar disorder as having created significant problems within the relationship and the symptomatic experience of bipolar disorder, such as behavioural hyperactivity and social withdrawal, was difficult to cope with.

Anticipate the need to use CBT techniques such as social skills training, cognitive restructuring, exposure therapy, and problemsolving training.

CBT techniques can be helpful for patients with bipolar disorder who are experiencing impaired social interaction by helping the patient develop coping strategies, improve social skills, and decrease social anxiety. A combination of CBT and psychoeducation has been described to be effective in terms of symptoms and social-occupational functioning improvement. Positive results in social functioning were also found with CBT.

Collaborate with other healthcare providers, such as psychiatrists and social workers. A multidisciplinary approach can provide patients with a more comprehensive treatment plan that addresses their physical, emotional, and social needs. The goal of treatment for patients with bipolar disorder is a full functional recovery or a return to pre-illness baseline functioning. This goal can best be achieved by integrating psychiatric and medical healthcare using an interprofessional team approach to manage bipolar disorder and comorbid psychiatric and medical conditions.

Reinforce information about psychological therapies designed to restore psychosocial functioning.

Several efforts have been made lately to design therapies to restore psychosocial functioning in bipolar disorder. The efficacy of functional remediation was proven in terms of improving functional outcomes in euthymic patients with moderate to severe functional impairment at baseline. Improvement in psychosocial functioning was maintained after a six-month follow-up. Functional remediation is especially centered on functional recovery, focusing on the training of neurocognitive skills that are useful for daily functioning. Encourage the patient to consume adequate and nutritious foods and to engage in physical exercise.

Nutrition and physical exercise play a critical role in both the mental and physical health of patients with bipolar disorder. Poor dietary habits and a sedentary lifestyle can increase physical and psychiatric morbidity, worsen psychosocial and cognitive functioning, and predict a poor pharmacological response.

Administer pharmacologic treatment as indicated.

A study tested the effects of lurasidone as monotherapy or as an adjunctive to lithium/valproate on health-related quality of life (HRQOL). They found that patients in both conditions increased HRQOL. Another study found that patients enhanced both their work functional outcome and QOL after receiving prophylactic lamotrigine therapy at a sixmonth follow-up.

3. Promoting Effective Coping

Patients with bipolar disorder may exhibit ineffective coping strategies due to biochemical and neurologic changes in the brain that affect their ability to regulate emotions and cope with stressors. In addition, disturbance in tension release and inadequate levels of perception of control may contribute to feelings of helplessness and exacerbate symptoms of the disorder. Furthermore, ineffective problem-solving strategies and poor coping skills can further complicate the patient's ability to manage their condition and lead to increased stress and mood instability. Families of patients with bipolar disorder may experience

disruption or impairment in the functioning and interactions within the family unit due to the potential for violence or aggressive behaviour from the patient during manic episodes.

Family members may also experience role shifts, where they take on additional caregiving responsibilities or have to navigate changes in family dynamics caused by the patient's condition. Nonadherence to medication regimens and situational crises, such as hospitalizations or financial strain, can also cause disruptions in family processes and relationships.

Assess and recognize early signs of manipulative behaviour, and intervene appropriately.

Setting limits is an important step in the intervention of bipolar patients, especially when intervening in manipulative behaviours. Staff agreement on limits set and consistency is imperative if the limits are to be carried out effectively. Examples of manipulative behaviour from the patient include taunting staff by pointing out faults or oversights; pitting one staff member against another or pitting one group against another; and aggressively demanding behaviours that can trigger exasperation and frustration in staff.

Observe for destructive behaviour toward self or others. Intervene in the early phases of escalation of manic behaviour.

Hostile verbal behaviours, poor impulse control, provocative behaviours, and violent acting out against others or property are some of the symptoms of this disease and are seen in extreme and/or acute mania. Aggression may include all acts of hostility toward becoming violent. Verbal aggression is very common and ranges from angry outbursts, loud shouts, and noises, to outright use of verbal threats without real physical harm. The patient's tone of voice can also be a warning sign of imminent violence. Early detection and intervention can prevent harm to the patient or others in the environment.

Study the behaviour of family members and friends

Studies of coping in bipolar disorder suggest that the way in which patients face the prodrome of mania and also their ability to recognize early signs of depression make a significant contribution to their level of social functioning. Patients diagnosed with bipolar disorder tend to use a less active and more avoidance-based style of coping in reaction to stress than people in the general population and exhibit a greater reliance on maladaptive coping strategies.

Observe for maladaptive coping strategies within the family.

Studies have shown that the family members of patients diagnosed with bipolar disorder have stress levels as high as those observed in the caregivers of people diagnosed with schizophrenia. Maladaptive coping strategies are observed in family environments marked by high levels of conflict and excessive control, and by low levels of cohesion and emotional support.

Maintain a firm, calm, and neutral approach at all times. Avoid arguing with the patient, getting involved in power struggles, and joking or "clever" repartee in response to the patient's "cheerful and humorous" mood.

These behaviours by the staff can escalate environmental stimulation and, consequently, manic activity. Once the manic patient is out of control, seclusion might be required, which can be traumatic to the manic individual as well as the staff. Healthcare personnel must be calm, confident, reassuring, and keep an open disposition. They should not challenge the patient's delusions or touch the patient. Reasoning with the patient can also invoke a violent response.

Have valuables, credit cards, and large sums of money sent home with family or put in the hospital safe until the patient is discharged.

During manic episodes, people give away valuables and money indiscriminately to strangers, often leaving themselves broke and in debt.

Research suggests about twothirds of people living with bipolar disorder will experience some grandiose delusion, such as running through their savings and buying expensive gifts for the family because the patient feels convinced that they are about to get a promotion and significant raise.

Provide hospital legal service when and if the patient is involved in making or signing important legal documents during an acute manic phase. Judgment and reality testing are both impaired during acute mania. Patients might need legal advice and protection against making important decisions that are not in their best interest. Introduce advanced decision-making (ADM) to the patient. This refers to people planning for a future when they may lose the capacity to make decisions about treatment. Patients with bipolar disorder may be particularly suited to using these new legal provisions, given the fluctuations in their decision-making process.

Administer mood stabilizers, as ordered, and evaluate for efficacy, and side and toxic effects.

Bipolar disorder is caused by biochemical/neurologic imbalances in the brain. Appropriate antimanic medications allow psychosocial and nursing interventions to be effective. Lithium is the drug commonly used for prophylaxis and treatment of manic episodes. However, this agent is also associated with an increased risk of reduced urinary concentrating ability, hypothyroidism, hyperparathyroidism, and weight gain. Lithium may also have some anti-suicidal action.

Prepare the patient for electroconvulsive therapy, as indicated.

Often, the severity of the patient's symptoms, the lack of response to medications, or the presence of contraindications to certain medications necessitates the use of ECT. this treatment modality has proven to be highly effective in the treatment of acute mania.

Advise the patient not to make changes in their salt intake.

Patients should be advised not to make significant changes in their salt intake, because increased salt intake may lead to reduced serum lithium levels and reduced efficacy, and reduced intake may lead to increased levels and toxicity.

Encourage the patient to exercise regularly.

Patients in the depressed phase are encouraged to exercise. These individuals should try to develop a regular daily schedule of major activities, especially times of going to bed and waking up. Propose a regular exercise schedule for all patients, especially those with bipolar disorder. Both exercise and a regular schedule are keys to surviving this illness.

Promote the use of positive coping skills.

Positive coping methods such as deep breathing exercises, relaxation activities, using problem-solving steps, and solving problems by discussion should be recommended to the patient. These techniques help reduce the patient's anxiety, calming them down and avoiding the progression to a manic state. Efforts should be made to ensure that the patient discovers their use of ineffective coping methods so that they can start with the process of utilizing positive ones.

Provide accurate information and honest answers.

Honest answers and accurate information facilitate the development of rapport. These enable the patient to use their own experiences and knowledge to make decisions. The patient may be told that their condition is really challenging and that they are supported by having positive feelings rather than negative ideas by confirming that they need to have a more helpful and realistic approach when they feel unwell.

Encourage verbalization of feelings and fears.

Accept the patient's statements in a non-judgemental manner when they verbalize their feelings. A non-judgemental approach may diminish the patient's fear, establish trust, provide opportunities to identify problems, and facilitate the problem-solving process. Patients should be encouraged to express their moods and ideas in an acceptable way.

An interview may be planned for that purpose.

Encourage friends and family members to support the patient in all aspects.

Social support is a key factor in helping participants in a study to manage the challenges of accepting a bipolar disorder diagnosis and coping with it. Eight participants reported that certain individuals within their social networks had helped them, for example by communicating their positive qualities to them. Others also reported that aspects of their bipolar-related recovery, such as feeling more emotionally stable, were associated with regaining control over some aspect of their social environment, such as carrying out usual activities with friends.

Identify individual roles and anticipated and perceived changes.

Responsibilities and roles may have to be partially or completely assumed by others, which can further complicate family coping. Studies have reported "parentification", which occurs when children are required to function as an adult when it is developmentally inappropriate for them to do so. These children are at an increased risk of developing a range of mental health difficulties as they get older and it can cause disruption to academic studies.

Identify and encourage the use of previously successful coping behaviours. This focuses on strengths and reaffirms an individual's ability to handle current roles. The more frequent use of the strategies of active coping, planning, positive reframing, and humour by the patient's relatives or caregivers provides indications of preserved cognitive function that could play a protective role against the development of psychiatric disorders. The more frequent use of the patient of strategies such as denial, self-distraction, and behavioural disengagement indicates a reduced capacity to manage adverse situations

that may be related to cognitive deterioration caused by disease duration.

Assess energy direction, whether efforts at problem-solving are purposeful or scattered.

The patient may need assistance to focus energies in an effective way to enhance coping. The use of venting exhibited an inverse relationship with age at the first episode, indicating that the younger the age at the first episode, the greater the frequency of venting coping. This finding in a study could suggest that this strategy is related to maturity and that the earlier in life the patients are affected by the mental disorder, the greater their use of emotional venting in response to stress.

Evaluate and discuss family goals and expectations.

The family may believe that all psychological interventions will bring about a cure. Despite accurate information, expectations may be unrealistic. Additionally, the patient's early recovery may be rapid, then plateau, resulting in disappointments and frustrations. In a study, the children in two-parent families often described their perception of the parent without bipolar and their role within the family. This enabled insight into family adjustment. During the first or second day of hospitalization, spend time with family identifying their needs during this time. This is a disease that can devastate and destroy some families. During an acute manic attack, families experience a great deal of disruption and confusion when their family members begin to act bizarrely, out of control, and at times aggressively. Families need to

understand the disease and what can and cannot be done to help control the disease, and where to go for help for their individual issues. It is necessary to investigate the manner in which patients and family members employ coping strategies and how to intervene to achieve better management of these factors, understanding which groups need interventions to help patients and relatives to better manage these situations. Encourage family members to participate in family therapy sessions to promote open communication and address any family dynamics issues.

Involving family members in therapy can help develop coping strategies and communication skills to manage potential crises and provide ongoing support for the patient. It is known that the family can be a protective factor or a risk factor for disease progression, depending on how conflicts are resolved.

Promote healthy coping mechanisms and stress reduction techniques for both the patient and family members such as exercise, mindfulness techniques, and engaging in creative activities. Other helpful strategies may include seeking social support, developing a daily routine, and avoiding alcohol and drug use. By providing coping mechanisms and stress reduction techniques, patients and family members can develop skills to handle emotions and enhance the ability to adjust to the struggles of bipolar disorder. This can help promote better mental health outcomes and improve the quality of life for all involved. The use of the acceptance coping strategy was directly related to age at the first episode: the greater the patient's age at the first episode, the more likely they were to employ acceptance coping. This type of coping is an adaptive strategy and comprises accepting that the stressful event has happened and is real, indicating greater awareness of the situation, which is needed to face up to it. The use of stress reduction techniques, helping patients and their families to modify the evaluation of stressful situations, can contribute to emotional improvement.

Collaborate with the patient's treatment team to ensure that medication regimens are followed and to address any concerns related to non-adherence.

Bipolar disorder is a chronic condition that requires ongoing treatment, including medication, to help treat symptoms and minimize the risk of relapse. Non-adherence with medication regimens can result in worsening symptoms and may increase the risk of hospitalization or other complications. Treatment of patients with bipolar disorder involves initial and ongoing patient education. To this end, a strong therapeutic alliance is essential.

Facilitate support groups or connect family members with local support groups to provide additional resources and a sense of community. Support groups can offer a safe space for patients and families to share experiences, receive emotional support, and learn from others who are going through the same

condition.

Encourage expression and acknowledgment of feelings.

Do not deny or assure the patient or family members that everything will be all right. Because it is not possible to predict the outcome, it is more helpful to assist the person to deal with feelings about what is happening instead of giving false reassurances. Stress the importance of continuous open dialogue between family members. This provides an opportunity to get feelings out in the open. Recognition and awareness

promote the resolution of guilt and anger. In a study, both patients and family noted that family primarily acted as a sounding board (talking through patient treatment preferences/feelings/concerns), which was a role more often assumed by partners/spouses than other family members.

Help the family recognize the needs of all members.

Attention may be so focused on the patient that other members feel isolated or abandoned, which can compromise family growth and unity. In a study about families with parents diagnosed with bipolar disorder, children were given additional responsibilities, and what was evident was the importance of support for these children, whether from another parent, extended family members, or friends. Having someone to talk to, support, distract, and be consistent was valued. Include family in consultations, care planning, and placement decisions. This facilitates communication, enables the family to be an integral part of the rehabilitation, and provides a sense of control. Two forms of family involvement may explain why family attendance was related to patients' achieving their involvement preferences. Firstly, the family provided clinicians with a comprehensive and personalized knowledge of the patient's circumstances. Secondly, families who attended consultations were better equipped to help patients clarify their understanding of and preferences for treatment.

Refer to family therapy and support groups.

Cognitive and personality changes are usually very difficult for the family to deal with. Decreased impulse control, emotional lability, and inappropriate sexual or aggressive and violent behaviour can disrupt family functioning and integrity. Trained therapists and peer role models may assist the family to deal with feelings and the reality of the situation and provide support for decisions that are made.

4. Assisting in Self-Care

Patients with bipolar disorder may experience a total self-care deficit due to the nature of the disorder, which can affect their ability to engage in self-care activities. This may be exacerbated during manic or depressive episodes, where patients may experience difficulties with hygiene, nutrition, and sleep. Additionally, medication side effects and cognitive impairments associated with the disorder may further impact their ability to engage in self-care activities.

Determine current capabilities using a 0 to 4 scale and barriers to participation in self-care.

A comprehensive functional assessment includes the independent performance of basic ADLs, social activities, sensory abilities, cognition, and the ability to ambulate. The use of the WHO Disability Assessment Schedule 2.0 (WHODAS 2.0) is recommended by the DSM-5. The WHODAS 2.0 allows the assessment of functioning and disability irrespective of diagnosis; that is, it can reflect difficulties due to any medical or psychiatric illness.

Providing adequate sleep

Keep the patient in areas of low stimulation.

This promotes relaxation and minimizes manic behaviour. Sleep disturbances are common in bipolar disorder, and a minimal stimuli environment can help the patient to improve their sleep quality this can be particularly important during manic or hypomanic episodes when the patient may have a decreased need for sleep.

Encourage frequent rest periods during the day. Patients diagnosed with bipolar disorder with abnormal sleep had similar mood symptoms to those with normal sleep but less stable biological rhythms, worse psychosocial functioning, and reduced quality of life. The patients with bipolar disorder in a study spent

longer in bed, had more fragmented sleep, and had more unstable and irregular sleepwake patterns.

At night, encourage warm baths, soothing music, and medication when indicated.

Avoid giving the patient caffeine.

This promotes relaxation, rest, and sleep. The patient should engage in a relaxing routine before bedtime, such as taking a warm bath, practicing relaxation techniques such as meditation or deep breathing, or reading a book. Stimulating activities such as watching TV or using electronic devices before bed should be avoided. Caffeine and alcohol can disrupt sleep, therefore, they must also be avoided, especially in the evenings.

Enhancing nutrition

Monitor intake, output, and vital signs. This ensures adequate fluid and caloric intake and minimizes dehydration and cardiac collapse. Poor diet habits can contribute to obesity, diabetes, hypertension, and

dyslipidemia, which in turn, increase the risk for cardiovascular disease. At any rate, these risk factors should be targeted since it has been shown that obesity can also impact cognitive functioning, and in turn, cognitive impairment can influence one another. Frequently remind the patient to eat. The manic patient is unaware of bodily needs and is easily distracted. Therefore, they need supervision to eat. A study noted that bipolar disorder patients report eating only one meal a day, eating alone, or having difficulty in obtaining or cooking food. Poor nutrition access or limited diet options for patients with bipolar disorder may directly contribute to poor diet quality. Encourage frequent high-calorie protein drinks and finger foods (e.g., sandwiches, fruit, protein shakes).

Constant fluid and calorie replacement are needed. The patient might be too active to sit at meals. Fingers foods allow "eating on the run". Studies showed that the diet scores showed more consumption of the Western-style dietary pattern and lower scores for a traditional dietary pattern (vegetables, fruit, chicken, lamb, fish, and whole-grain foods) among patients diagnosed with bipolar disorder. An unhealthy diet may actually cause or worsen bipolar disease.

Avoid giving the patient too many sugary foods and carbohydrates. A study found that patients diagnosed with bipolar disorder had a diet with higher energy intake and higher glycaemic load than controls. Another study found that bipolar patients consumed more total carbohydrates, sucrose, non-alcoholic beverages, sweetened drinks, cakes, and sweets. What these studies underscore is that bipolar patients tend to consume an unhealthier diet, and it is possible that poor diet quality may have a causative

role in bipolar disorder.

Provide vitamins and supplements to the patient as indicated.

Vitamin D and folate are essential for good neuronal functioning and have been shown to disorder. Folic acid and folate have been increasingly used in depressive disorders

Managing constipation

Monitor bowel habits; offer fluids and foods rich in fiber. Evaluate the need for a laxative. Encourage the patient to go to the bathroom. This prevents faecal impaction resulting from dehydration and decreased peristalsis.

There is growing evidence that mood disorders may be related to overall inflammation and

to changes in the microbiome, the bacteria that live in the digestive tract.

Assisting in grooming

If warranted, supervise choice of clothes; minimize flamboyant and bizarre dresses, and sexually suggestive dresses, such as bikini tops and bottoms. This lessens the potential for inappropriate attention, which can increase the level of mania, or ridicule, which lowers self-esteem and increases the need for manic defense.

This also assists the patient in maintaining dignity. Respondents in a study who needed some assistance in dressing were only able to choose and prepare the clothes to be used. They also needed assistance in determining the suitability of the clothes for the time. The patient's inability to fulfil these needs is influenced by the patient's awareness that they had not fully recovered so the patient still sometimes experiences disorientation toward reality. Therefore, the patient needs special guidance from the nurse to restore their basic abilities.

Give simple step-by-step reminders for hygiene and dress (e.g., "Here is your toothbrush. Put the toothpaste on the brush").

Distractability and poor concentration are countered by simple, concrete instructions. The nurse may discuss these with patients, check their needs for patient hygiene practices, and provide accurate and adequate information. This helps increase the level of independence from the partially assisted category to the independent category.

Arrange appointments for occupational therapy for the patient, as indicated.

Occupational therapy is the science and art of directing one's participation to carry out certain predetermined tasks. This therapy focuses on the introduction of abilities that still exist in a person, maintenance, and improvement aim to form a person to be independent, not dependent on the help of others. The purpose of this therapy is to restore mental function to create certain conditions so that the patient can develop the ability to be able to relate to other people and the surrounding community, as well as restore physical function, increase movement, muscles, and joints, and teach ADLs.

Encourage the patient to perform at an optimal level of function; however, do not rush the patient.

Encouragement promotes independence and a sense of control. It may also decrease feelings of helplessness. By giving directions to the patient to help themselves, improve their abilities, provide various activities to try and find out their mental and physical abilities, habits, social skills, direct talents, and hobbies to be used after the patient can become more independent.

CHAPTER V

PSYCHIATRIC NURSING IN ALCOHOL USE PROBLEMS

Alcohol withdrawal syndrome (AWS) is a common clinical condition that occurs in individuals with alcohol use disorder who abruptly stop or reduce their alcohol intake. It is characterized by a range of symptoms that can vary from mild to severe and potentially life-threatening. Nursing care plans for alcohol withdrawal are an essential part of managing patients with AWS. This article aims to provide an overview of nursing care plans for alcohol withdrawal nursing assessment, nursing diagnosis, including their nursing interventions, and nursing management.

What is Alcohol Withdrawal Syndrome?

Alcohol, a central nervous system depressant, is used socially in our society for many reasons: to enhance the flavour of food, to encourage relaxation and conviviality, for celebrations, and as a sacred ritual in some religious ceremonies. Therapeutically, it is the major ingredient in many OTC/ prescription medications. It can be harmless, enjoyable, and sometimes beneficial when used responsibly and in moderation. It is rapidly absorbed from the stomach and small intestine into the bloodstream. On the other hand, alcohol withdrawal refers to symptoms that may occur when a person who has been drinking too much alcohol every day suddenly stops drinking alcohol. Alcohol withdrawal symptoms usually occur within 8 hours after the last drink but can occur days later. Symptoms usually peak in 24 – 72 hours but may persist for weeks. Common symptoms include anxiety or nervousness, depression, fatigue, irritability, jumpiness or
shakiness, mood swings, nightmares and not thinking clearly.

Nursing Care Plans and Management

Nursing care plans for alcohol withdrawal are designed to support patients with AWS and ensure their safety and comfort during the withdrawal process. Nursing care planning for patients who are undergoing alcohol withdrawal includes: maintaining physiological stability during the acute withdrawal phase, promoting safety, providing appropriate referral and follow-up, and involvement of SO in the process.

Nursing Problem Priorities

The following are the nursing priorities for patients with alcohol withdrawal syndrome (AWS):

• Assessment and monitoring. Conducting a comprehensive assessment of the patient's alcohol withdrawal symptoms and closely monitoring vital signs, including heart rate, blood pressure, and respiratory rate.

• Seizure prevention. Implementing preventive measures, such as the administration of appropriate medications (e.g., benzodiazepines), to prevent seizures, a potential complication of alcohol withdrawal syndrome (AWS).

• Delirium tremens (DT) prevention. Identifying patients at high risk for delirium tremens and implementing interventions, including pharmacological support, to manage symptoms and reduce the risk of severe complications.

• Fluid and electrolyte balance. Monitoring and maintaining adequate fluid intake and electrolyte balance to prevent dehydration and address any imbalances caused by AWS.

• Pharmacologic support. Administering medications, such as benzodiazepines or anticonvulsants, to manage alcohol withdrawal symptoms, including anxiety, agitation, insomnia, and tremors.

• Psychological support. Providing psychological support, counselling, and behavioural interventions to address the emotional and psychological challenges associated with AWS, including cravings, depression, anxiety, and mood disturbances.

• Nutritional support. Ensuring proper nutrition and addressing any nutritional deficiencies caused by alcohol abuse and poor dietary habits.

• Safety measures. Implementing safety protocols to prevent self-harm, falls, or accidents during the withdrawal process, including close observation and removing any potentially harmful objects from the patient's environment.

• Education and relapse prevention. Providing education on the consequences of alcohol abuse, promoting awareness of triggers and coping strategies, and offering relapse prevention strategies to support longterm recovery. Discharge planning. Collaborating with the patient, family, and support networks to develop a comprehensive discharge plan that includes appropriate follow-up care, referrals to rehabilitation programs or support groups, and ongoing monitoring of the patient's progress in managing AWS and maintaining sobriety.

Nursing Assessment

Assess for the following subjective and objective data:

Nursing Diagnosis

Following a thorough assessment, a nursing diagnosis is formulated to specifically address the challenges associated with alcohol withdrawal syndrome (AWS) based on the nurse's clinical judgment and understanding of the patient's unique health condition. While nursing diagnoses serve as a framework for organizing care, their usefulness may vary in different clinical situations. In real-life clinical settings, it is important to note that the use of specific nursing diagnostic labels may not be as prominent or commonly

utilized as other components of the care plan. It is ultimately the nurse's clinical expertise and judgment that shape the care plan to meet the unique needs of each patient, prioritizing their health concerns and priorities.

Nursing Goals

Goals and expected outcomes may include:

• The patient will verbalize the reduction of fear and anxiety to an acceptable and manageable level.

• The patient will express a sense of regaining some control of the situation/life.

• The patient will demonstrate problem-solving skills and use resources effectively.

• The patient will regain/maintain the usual level of consciousness.

• The patient will report the absence of/reduced hallucinations.

• The patient will identify external factors that affect sensory-perceptual abilities.

• The patient will display vital signs within the patient's normal range; absence of/reduced frequency of dysrhythmias.

• The patient will demonstrate an increase in activity tolerance.

• The patient will maintain an effective breathing pattern with a respiratory rate within normal range, lungs clear; be free of cyanosis and other signs/symptoms of hypoxia.

• The patient will demonstrate the absence of untoward effects of withdrawal.

• The patient will experience no physical injury.

Nursing Interventions and Actions

Therapeutic interventions and nursing actions for patients with alcohol withdrawal syndrome (AWS) may include:

1. Managing Signs of Alcohol Withdrawal Syndrome

- Patients with alcohol withdrawal may experience sensory perceptual changes due to a combination of factors, including chronic alcohol consumption, sleep deprivation, and psychological stress. These factors can contribute to alterations in the patient's perception of their surroundings, such as visual or auditory hallucinations, as well as difficulties in clear thinking and information processing.
- Additionally, patients with alcohol withdrawal are susceptible to decreased cardiac output, which may occur as a direct consequence of alcohol's impact on the heart muscle, resulting in damage and impaired function. It can also cause changes in systemic vascular resistance, affecting blood flow and cardiac performance. In severe cases, reduced cardiac output can lead to complications like hypotension, shock, and organ failure.
- Moreover, patients with alcohol withdrawal are prone to impaired respiratory function caused by tracheobronchial obstruction, which can arise from incidents involving aspiration or choking. Furthermore, alcohol toxicity depresses the central nervous system and impairs respiratory function, which can contribute to various respiratory complications, including hypoxemia and respiratory failure.
- Assess the level of consciousness; ability to speak, and respond to stimuli and commands.
- Speech may be garbled, confused, or slurred. Response to commands may reveal an inability to concentrate, impaired judgment, or muscle coordination deficits. Observe behavioural responses such as hyperactivity, disorientation, confusion, sleeplessness, and irritability.
- Hyperactivity related to CNS disturbances may escalate rapidly. Sleeplessness is common due to the loss of the sedative effect gained from alcohol usually consumed before bedtime. Sleep deprivation may aggravate disorientation and confusion. Progression of symptoms may indicate impending hallucinations (stage II) or DTs (stage III). Note the onset of hallucinations. Document as auditory, visual, and tactile. Auditory hallucinations are reported to be more frightening and threatening to the patient.
- Visual hallucinations occur more at night and often include insects, animals, or the faces of friends and enemies. Patients are frequently observed "picking the air." Yelling may occur if the patient is calling for

help from a perceived threat (usually seen in stage III AWS).

- Monitor the patient for signs of depression.
- To avoid harming himself and attempts suicide.
- Monitor laboratory studies: electrolytes, magnesium levels, liver function studies, ammonia, BUN, glucose, and ABGs.
- Changes in organ function may precipitate or potentiate sensory-perceptual deficits. Electrolyte imbalance is common. Liver function is often impaired in the chronic alcoholic, and ammonia intoxication can occur if the liver is unable to convert ammonia to urea. Ketoacidosis is sometimes present without glycosuria; however, hyperglycaemia or hypoglycaemia may occur, suggesting pancreatitis or impaired gluconeogenesis in the liver.
- Hypoxemia and hypercarbia are common manifestations in chronic alcoholics who are also heavy smokers.
- Provide a calm environment, minimizing noise and shadows.
- To reduce the incidence of delusions and hallucinations.
- Avoid restraining the patient unless necessary.
- To protect patients and others.
- Provide a quiet environment. Speak in a calm, quiet voice. Regulate lighting as indicated. Turn off the radio and TV during sleep.
- Reduces external stimuli during the hyperactive stage. Patients may become more delirious when their surroundings cannot be seen, but some respond better to quiet, darkened rooms.
- Provide care by the same staff whenever possible.
- Promotes recognition of caregivers and a sense of consistency, which may reduce fear.
- Encourage SO to stay with the patient whenever possible.
- May have a calming effect, and may provide a reorienting influence.
- Reorient frequently to person, place, time, and surrounding environment as indicated.
- May reduce confusion, and prevent and limit misinterpretation of external stimuli.
- Avoid bedside discussion about the patient or topics unrelated to the patient that does not include the patient.
- Patients may hear and misinterpret conversation, which can aggravate hallucinations.
- Provide environmental safety (place bed in a low position, leave doors in a fully open or closed position, observe frequently, place call light or bell

within reach, remove articles that can harm the patient).

- Patients may have a distorted sense of reality or be fearful or suicidal, requiring protection from self.
- Provide seclusion, and restraints as necessary.
- Patients with excessive psychomotor activity, severe hallucinations, violent behaviour, and suicidal gestures may respond better to seclusion. Restraints are usually ineffective and add to the patient's agitation, but occasionally may be required to prevent self-harm.
- Orient the patient to reality.
- Patients may experience hallucinations and may try to harm themselves and others.
- Administer medications as indicated: Antianxiety agents as indicated
- Reduces hyperactivity, promoting relaxation and sleep. Drugs that have little effect on dreaming may be desired to allow dream recovery (REM rebound) to occur, which has previously been suppressed by alcohol use.
- Monitor vital signs frequently during acute withdrawal.
- Hypertension frequently occurs in the acute withdrawal phase. Extreme hyperexcitability, accompanied by catecholamine release and increased peripheral vascular resistance, raises BP and heart rate; however, BP may become labile and progress to hypotension. Note: The patient may have underlying cardiovascular disease, which is compounded by alcohol withdrawal.
- Monitor cardiac rate and rhythm. Document irregularities and dysrhythmias.
- Long-term alcohol abuse may result in cardiomyopathy or HF. Tachycardia is common because of the sympathetic response to increased circulating catecholamines.
- Irregularities and dysrhythmias may develop with electrolyte shifts and imbalance. All of these may have an adverse effect on cardiac function and output.
- Monitor body temperature.
- Elevation may occur because of sympathetic stimulation, dehydration, and infections, causing vasodilation and compromising venous return and cardiac output.
- Monitor I&O. Note 24-hr fluid balance.
- Preexisting dehydration, vomiting, fever, and diaphoresis may result in decreased circulating volume that can compromise cardiovascular function. Note: Hydration is difficult to assess in the alcoholic patient

because the usual indicators are not reliable, and overhydration is a risk in the presence of compromised cardiac function.

- Monitor laboratory studies: serum electrolyte levels.
- Electrolyte imbalance: potassium, and magnesium, potentiate the risk of cardiac dysrhythmias and CNS excitability.
- Be prepared and assist in cardiopulmonary resuscitation.
- Causes of death during acute withdrawal stages include cardiac dysrhythmias, respiratory depression and arrest, oversedation, excessive psychomotor activity, severe dehydration or overhydration, and massive infections. Mortality for unrecognized and untreated delirium tremens (DTs) may be as high as 25%.
- Administer fluids and electrolytes, as indicated.
- Severe alcohol withdrawal causes the patient to be susceptible to fluid losses (associated with fever, diaphoresis, and vomiting) and electrolyte imbalances, especially potassium, magnesium, and glucose.
- Administer medications as indicated: Clonidine (Catapres), atenolol (Tenormin); Potassium.
- Although the use of benzodiazepines is often sufficient to control hypertension during initial withdrawal from alcohol, some patients may require more specific therapy. Note: Atenolol and other b-adrenergic blockers may speed up the withdrawal process and eliminate tremors, as well as lower the heart rate, blood pressure, and body temperature.
- Correct deficits that can result in life-threatening dysrhythmias.
- Monitor respiratory rate and depth and pattern as indicated. Note periods of apnoea, and Cheyne-Stokes respirations.
- Frequent assessment is important because toxicity levels may change rapidly.
- Hyperventilation is common during the acute withdrawal phase. Kussmaul's respirations are sometimes present because of an acidotic state associated with vomiting and malnutrition. However, marked respiratory depression can occur because of the CNS depressant effects of alcohol if acute intoxication is present. This may be compounded by drugs used to control alcohol withdrawal symptoms (AWS).
- Auscultate breath sounds. Note the presence of adventitious sounds: rhonchi, wheezes.
- The patient is at risk for atelectasis related to hypoventilation and pneumonia. Right lower lobe pneumonia is common in alcohol-debilitated patients and is often due to chronic aspiration. Chronic lung

diseases are also common: emphysema and bronchitis.

- Review serial chest x-rays, ABGs, and pulse oximetry as available and indicated
- Monitors the presence of secondary complications such as atelectasis and pneumonia; evaluates the effectiveness of respiratory effort, identifies therapy needs.
- Elevate the head of the bed.
- Decreases potential for aspiration; lowers diaphragm, enhancing lung inflation.
- Encourage cough and deep-breathing exercises and frequent position changes.
- Facilitates lung expansion and mobilization of secretions to reduce the risk of atelectasis and pneumonia.
- Have suction equipment, and airway adjuncts available.
- The sedative effects of alcohol and drugs potentiate the risk of aspiration, relaxation of oropharyngeal muscles, and respiratory depression, requiring intervention to prevent respiratory arrest.
- Administer supplemental oxygen if necessary.
- Hypoxia may occur with CNS and respiratory depression.

2. Promoting Safety and Preventing Injury and Seizures

- Patients with alcohol withdrawal are at risk for injury due to a variety of factors, including sudden cessation of alcohol, which can lead to severe physiological symptoms, such as seizures. Reduced hand and eye coordination, balancing difficulties, and confusion can also increase the risk of falls and other accidents, which can lead to serious injury.
- Additionally, some patients may engage in risky or impulsive behaviours as a result of their altered state of mind, further increasing the risk of injury.
- Identify the stage of AWS (alcohol withdrawal syndrome); i.e., stage I is associated with signs and symptoms of hyperactivity (tremors, sleeplessness, nausea and vomiting, diaphoresis, tachycardia, hypertension).
- Stage II is manifested by increased hyperactivity plus hallucinations and seizure activity. Stage III symptoms include DTs and extreme autonomic hyperactivity with profound confusion, anxiety, insomnia, and fever.

- Prompt recognition and intervention may halt the progression of symptoms and enhance recovery or improve prognosis. In addition, the recurrence or progression of symptoms indicates the need for changes in drug therapy and more intense treatment to prevent death.
- Monitor and document seizure activity. Maintain patent airway. Provide environmental safety (padded side rails, bed in low position). Grand mal seizures are most common and may be related to decreased magnesium levels, hypoglycaemia, elevated blood alcohol, or a history of head trauma and preexisting seizure disorder. Note: In absence of history and other pathology causing seizures, they usually stop spontaneously, requiring only symptomatic treatment.
- **Note: Antiepileptic drugs are not indicated for alcohol withdrawal seizures.**
- Check deep-tendon reflexes. Assess gait, if possible.
- Reflexes may be depressed, absent, or hyperactive. Peripheral neuropathies are common, especially in malnourished patients. Ataxia (gait disturbance) is associated with Wernicke's syndrome (thiamine deficiency) and cerebellar degeneration.
- Assist with ambulation and self-care activities as needed.
- Prevents falls with resultant injury.
- Provide for environmental safety when indicated.
- May be required when equilibrium, hand, and eye coordination problems exist.

3. Reducing Fear and Anxiety

- Patients with alcohol withdrawal are at risk for anxiety and fear related to the cessation of alcohol intake and physiological withdrawal symptoms. Hospitalization and the threat to self-concept can further exacerbate these feelings, as patients may feel a loss of control over their own lives and worry about the impact of their condition on their relationships and daily activities.
- Determine the cause of anxiety, involving the patient in the process. Explain that alcohol withdrawal increases anxiety and uneasiness. Reassess the level of anxiety on an ongoing basis.
- A person in the acute phase of withdrawal may be unable to identify and accept what is happening. Anxiety may be physiologically or environmentally caused. Continued alcohol toxicity will be manifested

by increased anxiety and agitation as the effects of the medication wear off.

Monitor the patient for signs of depression.

- To prevent suicidal attempts.
- Develop a trusting relationship through frequent contact being honest and nonjudgmental. Project an accepting attitude about alcoholism.
- Provides patient with a sense of humanness, helping to decrease paranoia and distrust.
- Patients will be able to detect the biased or condescending attitudes of caregivers.
- Maintain a calm environment, minimizing noise.
- Reduces stress.
- Inform the patient about what you plan to do and why. Include patients in the planning process and provide choices when possible.
- Enhances a sense of trust, and explanation may increase cooperation and reduce anxiety. Provides a sense of control over self in circumstances where the loss of control is a significant factor. Note: Feelings of self-worth are intensified when one is treated as a worthwhile person.
- Reorient frequently.
- The patient may experience periods of confusion, resulting in increased anxiety.
- Orient the patient to reality.
- He may also experience hallucinations and may try to harm himself and others.
- Administer medications as indicated.
- Arrange "Intervention" (confrontation) in a controlled setting.
- Process wherein SO and family members, supported by staff, provide information about how the patient's drinking and behaviour have affected each one of them, helps the patient acknowledge that drinking is a problem and has resulted in the current situational crisis.
- Provide consultation for referral to detoxification and crisis center for ongoing treatment programs as soon as medically stable (oriented to reality).
- The patient is more likely to contract treatment while still hurting and experiencing fear and anxiety from the last drinking episode. Motivation decreases as well-being increases and the person again feel able to

control the problem. Direct contact with available treatment resources provides a realistic picture of help. Decreases time for patients to "think about it," change minds or restructure and strengthen denial systems.

4. Initiating Patient Education and Health Teachings

- These nursing interventions aim to empower patients with knowledge and skills to manage their alcohol withdrawal syndrome effectively and promote successful recovery.
- Provide thorough education to patients with AWS regarding the physical and psychological effects of alcohol withdrawal, including symptoms, risks, and potential complications.
- Providing education about the physical and psychological effects of alcohol withdrawal helps patients understand what to expect during the process, reducing anxiety and increasing their motivation to stay committed to treatment.
- Teach patients healthy coping mechanisms and stress management techniques, such as deep breathing exercises, mindfulness techniques, and engaging in activities that promote relaxation.
- Teaching patients healthy coping strategies and stress management techniques equips them with effective tools to manage triggers and cravings, reducing the likelihood of relapse and promoting long-term recovery.
- Educate patients about available support systems, such as Alcoholics Anonymous (AA) or other support groups, counselling services, and community resources, and encourage their participation to enhance their recovery journey.
- Educating patients about available support systems and resources, such as support groups and counselling services, helps them establish a strong support network, providing encouragement, guidance, and a sense of belonging during their recovery journey.
- Explain the importance of medication adherence in managing AWS and provide clear instructions on the prescribed medications, their purpose, potential side effects, and proper dosage. Emphasize the significance of following the prescribed medication regimen and attending scheduled medical appointments for monitoring and adjustment of treatment if necessary.

- Providing clear instructions on medication use and emphasizing the importance of adherence ensures that patients receive the full benefits of prescribed medications, reducing withdrawal symptoms and minimizing the risk of complications. Regular monitoring allows for adjustments to the treatment plan, ensuring its effectiveness.

- Provide education on the importance of a balanced diet, adequate hydration, and regular physical activity to support overall health and recovery. Discuss the negative effects of alcohol on nutrition and encourage healthy habits, such as consuming nutritious meals, avoiding alcohol, and staying hydrated.

- Educating patients about the impact of alcohol on nutrition and overall health helps them recognize the importance of a balanced diet, hydration, and regular physical activity in supporting their recovery. This knowledge empowers patients to make healthier lifestyle choices and promotes overall well-being.

5. Administer Medications and Provide Pharmacologic Support

- Benzodiazepines: Oxazepam, Lorazepam, chlordiazepoxide (Librium), diazepam (Valium): Antianxiety agents are given during acute withdrawal to help the patient relax, be less hyperactive, and feel more in control.BZDs are commonly used to control neuronal hyperactivity because of their minimal respiratory and cardiac depression and anticonvulsant properties. Studies have also shown that these drugs can prevent progression to more severe states of withdrawal. IV and PO administration is the preferred route because IM absorption is unpredictable. Muscle-relaxant qualities are particularly helpful to patients in controlling "the shakes," trembling, and ataxic quality of movements. Patients may initially require large doses to achieve the desired effect, and then drugs may be tapered and discontinued, usually within 96 hr. Note: These agents are used cautiously in patients with known hepatic disease because they are metabolized by the liver, although Serax has a shorter half-life.

- Haloperidol (Haldol): May be used in conjunction with BZDs for patients experiencing hallucinations or for delirium.

- Thiamine: 100mg parenteral Thiamine bolus dose must be given first to any patient suspected of Alcohol related withdrawal to prevent worsening of withdrawal, seizures and to prevent neuritis, Wernecke's syndrome, and Korsakoff's psychosis.

- Magnesium sulfate: Reduces tremors and seizure activity by decreasing neuromuscular excitability.
- Quetiapine: Quetiapine 100mg to 300mg can be used without problem for sleep disturbances in addition to the benzodiazepines.

CHAPTER VI

PSYCHIATRIC NURSING IN DEMENTIA

Dementia is a progressive neurological disorder that impairs cognitive function, affecting an individual's memory, thinking, reasoning, and daily functioning. It is not a single disease but rather an umbrella term that encompasses a range of conditions characterized by the decline of cognitive abilities beyond what is considered normal aging. The condition exerts a great impact not only on individuals but also on their families, caregivers, and society at large.

As the global population ages, understanding dementia becomes increasingly essential for nurses. This nursing note discusses into the various aspects of dementia, highlighting its causes, symptoms, diagnosis, medical management, and nursing interventions. Dementia is a term used to describe a group of progressive neurological disorders that result in a decline in cognitive function and memory. It affects thinking, behaviour, and the ability to perform daily activities. It often results from underlying medical conditions, substance use, or medication effects. It has a slow, insidious onset, and is chronic, progressive, and irreversible.

Statistics and Incidences

Cases of dementia are increasing due to the longer life expectancy of the world population.

• There are four clinical dementia syndromes accounting for 90% of all cases after excluding other common reversible causes of cognitive impairment.

• The rise in dementia and Alzheimer's disease is alarming and is expected to double every 20 years, from 47 million people in 2015 to 75 million people in 2030 and 131 million in 2050.

Causes

The following are major etiologic categories for the syndrome of dementia:

• **Dementia of the Alzheimer's type.** The exact disease of Alzheimer's disease is unknown, but several theories have been proposed, such as reduction in brain acetylcholine, the formation of plaques and tangles, serious head trauma, and genetic factors. Pathologic changes in the brain include atrophy, enlarged ventricles, and the presence of numerous neurofibrillary plaques and tangles.

• **Vascular Dementia.** This type of dementia is caused by significant cerebrovascular disease. The patient suffers the equivalent of small strokes caused by arterial hypertension or cerebral emboli or thrombi, which destroy many areas of the brain. The onset of symptoms is more abrupt than in AD and runs a highly variable course, progressing in steps rather than a gradual deterioration.

• **Dementia due to HIV disease.** The immune dysfunction associated with human immunodeficiency virus (HIV) can lead to brain infections by other organisms. HIV also appears to cause dementia directly.

• Dementia due to head trauma. The syndrome of symptoms associated with dementia can be brought on by a traumatic head injury.

• **Dementia due to Lewy Body Disease.** Clinically, Lewy Body disease is fairly similar to AD,; however, it tends to progress more rapidly, and there is an earlier appearance of visual hallucinations and Parkinsonian features (Rabins et al, 2006). This disorder is distinctive by the presence of Lewy bodies-eosinophilic inclusion bodies- seen in the cerebral cortex and brainstem (Andreasen and Black, 2006).

• **Dementia due to Parkinson's disease.** Parkinson's disease is caused by a loss of nerve cells in the substantia nigra of the basal ganglia. The symptoms of dementia associated with Parkinson's disease closely
resemble those of AD.

• **Dementia due to Huntington's disease.** This disease is transmitted as a Mendelian dominant gene, and damage occurs in the areas of the basal ganglia and the cerebral cortex.

• Dementia due to Pick's disease. Pathology occurs from atrophy in the frontal and temporal lobes of the brain. Symptoms are strikingly similar to those of AD, and Pick's disease is often misdiagnosed as AD.

• **Dementia due to Creutzfeldt-Jakob disease.** This form of dementia is caused by a transmissible agent known as a "slow virus" or prion. The clinical presentation is typical of the syndrome of dementia and the course is extremely rapid, with progressive deterioration and death within one year after onset.

• **Dementia due to other general medical conditions.** A number of other general medical conditions can cause dementia. Some of these include endocrine conditions, pulmonary disease, hepatic or renal failure,
cardiopulmonary insufficiency, fluid and electrolyte imbalances, nutritional deficiencies, frontal or temporal lobe lesions, uncontrolled epilepsy, central nervous system or systemic infections, and other neurological conditions.

• **Substance-induced Persisting Dementia.** This type of dementia is related to the persisting effects of substances such as alcohol, inhalants, sedatives, hypnotics, anxiolytics, other medications, and environmental toxins.

Clinical Manifestations

The following symptoms have been identified with the syndrome of dementia:

• *Memory impairment. Impaired ability to learn new information or to recall previously learned information.*

• *Impairment in abstract thinking, judgment, and impulse control.*

• *Impairment in language ability, such as difficulty naming objects. In some instances, the individual may not speak at all (aphasia).*

• *Personality changes are common.*

• *Impaired ability to perform motor activities despite intact motor abilities (apraxia).*

• *Disorientation. Patients may feel disoriented regarding their current place, time, o names of persons they are close with.*

• *Wandering. Because of disorientation, patients with dementia may often wander from one place to another.*

• *Delusions are common (particularly delusions of persecution).*

Assessment and Diagnostic Findings

Laboratory tests can be performed to rule out other conditions that may cause cognitive impairment.

• **Complete blood cell count (CBC).** Abnormalities in complete blood cell count and cobalamin levels require further workup to rule out hematologic disease.

• **Liver enzyme levels.** Abnormalities found in screening of liver enzyme levels require further workup to rule out hepatic disease.

• **Thyroid-stimulating hormone (TSH) levels.** Abnormalities in thyroidstimulating hormone levels require further workup to rule out thyroid disease.

• **Rapid plasma reagent.** Abnormalities in rapid plasma reagent (RPR) require further workup to rule out syphilis.

• **HIV serology.** Abnormalities in HIV serology and/or PCR require further workup to rule out HIV/AIDS.

• **Paraneoplastic antibodies.** Abnormalities in paraneoplastic antibodies require further workup to rule out autoimmune encephalitis.

• **CSF proteins.** Abnormalities in CSF proteins tau, P-tau, and 14-3-3 require further workup to rule out Creutzfeldt-Jakob disease.

Medical Management

To date, only symptomatic therapies are available and thus do not act on the evolution of the disease.

Experimental therapies. A variety of experimental therapies have been proposed for dementia; these include anti-amyloid therapy, reversal of excess tau phosphorylation, estrogen therapy, vitamin E therapy, and free radical scavenger therapy; however, the results of these studies have yielded disappointing results.

• **Dietary measures.** There are no special dietary considerations for dementia; however, caprylidene (Axona) is a prescription medical food that is metabolized into ketone bodies, and the brain can use these ketone bodies for energy when its ability to process glucose is impaired. Brainimaging scans of older adults and persons with dementia reveal a dramatically decreased uptake of glucose.

• **Physical activity.** Routine physical activity and exercise may have an impact on dementia progression and may perhaps have a protective effect on brain health; the patient's surroundings should be safe and familiar; maintaining structured routines may be helpful to decrease patient's stress in regard to meals, medication, and other therapeutic activities aimed at maintaining cognitive functioning.

Pharmacological management

The mainstay of therapy for patients with dementia is the use of centrally acting cholinesterase inhibitors to attempt to compensate for the depletion of acetylcholine in the cerebral cortex and hippocampus.

• Cholinesterase inhibitors. Cholinesterase inhibitors are used to palliate cholinergic deficiency.

• N-Methyl-D-Aspartate antagonists. The only drug in the N-methyl-Daspartate (NMDA) antagonist class that is approved by the US Food and Drug Administration is memantine; this agent may be used alone or in combination with AChE inhibitors.

• Nutritional supplement. Medical foods are dietary supplements intended to compensate specific nutritional problems caused by a disease or condition; caprylidene is indicated for clinical dietary management of metabolic processes associated with mild to moderate dementia.

Nursing Management

The nursing management of a patient with dementia includes the following:

Nursing Assessment

Assessment of a patient with dementia includes the following:

• Psychiatric interview. The psychiatric interview must contain a description of the patient's mental status with a thorough description of behaviour, flow of thought and speech, affect, thought processes and mental content, sensorium and intellectual resources, cognitive status, insight, and judgment.

• Serial assessment. Serial assessment of psychiatric status is necessary for determining the fluctuating course and acute changes in mental status, interviews with family members should be included and can be crucial in the treatment of infants and young children with cognitive disorders.

Nursing Diagnosis

Nursing diagnoses that you can use for developing nursing care plans for patients with dementia include:

• Risk for trauma related to disorientation or confusion.

• Risk for self-directed or other-directed violence related to delusional thinking.

• Chronic confusion related to alteration in structure/function of brain tissue.

• Self-care deficit related to cognitive impairment.

• Risk for falls related to cognitive impairment.

Nursing Care Planning and Goals

The major nursing care planning goals for dementia are:

• The patient will accept explanations of inaccurate interpretations within the environment.

• With assistance from the caregiver, the patient will be able to interrupt nonreality-based thinking.

Nursing Interventions

The nursing interventions for a dementia patient are:

• *Orient patient.* Frequently orient the patient to reality and surroundings. Allow the patient to have familiar objects around him or her; use other items, such as a clock, a calendar, and daily schedules, to assist in maintaining reality orientation.

• *Encourage caregivers about patient reorientation.* Teach prospective caregivers how to orient patients to time, person, place, and circumstances, as required. These caregivers will be responsible for patient safety after discharge from the hospital.

• *Enforce positive feedback.* Give positive feedback when thinking and behaviour are appropriate, or when the patient verbalizes that certain ideas expressed are not based in reality. Positive feedback increases selfesteem and enhances the desire to repeat appropriate behaviour. *Explain simply.* Use simple explanations and face-to-face interaction when communicating with patients. Do not shout messages into the patient's ear.

Speaking slowly and in a face-to-face position is most effective when communicating with an elderly individual experiencing hearing loss.

• *Discourage suspiciousness of others*. Express reasonable doubt if the patient relays suspicious beliefs in response to delusional thinking. Discuss with the patient the potential personal negative effects of continued suspiciousness of others.

• *Avoid the cultivation of false ideas.* Do not permit the rumination of false ideas. When this begins, talk to the patient about real people and real events.

• *Observe the patient closely.* Close observation of the patient's behaviour is indicated if delusional thinking reveals an intention for violence. Patient safety is a nursing priority.

Evaluation

The outcome criteria for a patient with dementia include:

• With assistance from the caregiver, the patient is able to distinguish between reality-based and non-reality-based thinking.

• Prospective caregivers are able to verbalize ways in which to orient patients to reality, as needed.

Documentation Guidelines

Documentation needed for a patient with dementia include the following:

• Individual findings, including factors affecting, interactions, nature of social exchanges, specifics of individual behaviour.

• Cultural and religious beliefs, and expectations.

• Plan of care.

• Teaching plan.

• Responses to interventions, teaching, and actions performed.

• Attainment or progress toward the desired outcome.

CHAPTER VII

PSYCHIATRIC NURSING IN ANXIETY DISORDERS AND PANIC DISORDERS

What are Anxiety Disorders?

Anxiety disorders involve disorders that contain characteristics of excessive fear and anxiety and linked behavioural disturbances. It manifests as a prolonged and dysfunctional reaction to stress, influenced by variations in one's genetic predisposition, developmental factors, and life experiences.

Types of Anxiety Disorders

The characteristic features of this group of disorders are symptoms of anxiety and avoidance behaviour. Anxiety disorders are categorized in the following manner:

- *Panic disorder (with or without agoraphobia).* Panic disorder is characterized by recurrent panic attacks, the onset of which are unpredictable, and manifested by intense apprehension, fear or terror, often associated with feelings of impending doom, and accompanied by intense physical discomfort.

- *Agoraphobia without history of panic disorder.* The APA 2000 Diagnostic and Statistical Manual of Mental Disorders, Fourth Edition, Text Revision (DSM-IV-TR) identifies the essential feature of this disorder as fear of being in places or situations from which escape might be difficult or in which help might not be available in the event of suddenly developing a symptom(s) that could be incapacitating or extremely embarrassing.

- *Social phobia.* Social phobia is characterized by a persistent fear of behaving or performing in the presence of others in a way that will be humiliating or embarrassing to the individual.

- *Specific phobia.* Formerly called simple phobia, this disorder is characterized by persistent fears of specific objects or situations.

- *Obsessive-compulsive disorder.* This disorder is characterized by involuntary recurring thoughts or images that the individual is unable to ignore and by recurring impulse to perform a seemingly purposeless activity.

- ***Posttraumatic stress disorder.*** Posttraumatic stress disorder is characterized by the development of physiological and behavioural symptoms following a psychologically traumatic event that is generally outside the range of usual human experience.
- ***Acute stress disorder.*** Acute stress disorder is characterized by the development of physiological and behavioural symptoms similar to those of PTSD; the major difference in the diagnosis lies in the length of time the symptoms exist; with acute stress disorder, the symptoms must subside within 4 weeks of occurrence of the stressor.
- ***Anxiety disorder due to a general medical condition.*** The symptoms of this disorder are judged to be the direct physiological consequence of a general medical condition.
- ***Substance-induced anxiety disorder.*** The DSM-IV-TR (APA, 2000) describes the essential features of this disorder as prominent anxiety symptoms that are judged to be caused by the direct physiological effects of a substance.

Obsessive-compulsive disorder (included in the obsessive-compulsive and related disorders), posttraumatic stress disorder (included in the trauma and stress-related disorders), and acute stress disorder, are no longer considered anxiety disorders as they were in the previous version of the DSM. Nonetheless, these disorders are closely linked to anxiety disorders and the sequential order of these chapters in the DSM-5 reflects this close connection.

Clinical Manifestations

Signs and symptoms of anxiety disorders may include the following:

- Pounding, rapid heart rate.
- Feeling of choking or smothering.
- Difficulty breathing.
- Pain in the chest.
- Feeling dizzy or faint.
- Increased perspiration.
- Feeling of numbness or tingling in the extremities.
- Trembling.
- Fear that one is dying or going crazy.
- Sense of impending doom.
- Feelings of unreality (derealization and/or depersonalization).

Assessment and Diagnostic Findings

For presentations with a higher index of suspicion for other medical causes of anxiety, more detailed evaluations may be indicated to identify or exclude underlying medical disorders.

- EEG, lumbar puncture, and head/brain imaging. Rule out CNS disorder using EEG, lumbar puncture, and brain computed tomography scan, as indicated by history and associated clinical findings.
- Electrocardiography. Rule out cardiac disorders using electrocardiography or treadmill ECG.
- Tests for infection. Rule out infectious causes using rapid plasma reagent test, lumbar puncture, or HIV testing.
- Arterial blood gas analysis. Arterial blood gas analysis is useful in confirming hyperventilation and excluding hypoxemia or metabolic acidosis.
- Chest radiography. Chest radiography is useful in excluding other causes of dyspnoea with chest pain.
- Thyroid function. Hyperthyroidism is one of the most common medical causes of anxiety related to a medical condition.

Medical Management

Treatment usually consists of a combination of pharmacotherapy and/or psychotherapy. **Cognitive therapy.** Cognitive therapy helps patients understand how automatic thoughts and false beliefs/distortions lead to exaggerated emotional responses, such as anxiety, and can lead to secondary behavioural consequences. **Behavioural therapy.** Behavioural therapy involves sequentially greater exposure of the patient to anxiety-provoking stimuli, over time, the patient becomes desensitized to the experience. **Diet.** Caffeine-containing products, such as coffee, tea, and colas, should be discontinued.

Pharmacologic Management

Antidepressant agents are the drugs of choice in the treatment of anxiety disorders, particularly the newer agents that have a safer adverse effect profile and higher ease of use than the older tricyclic antidepressants. **Selective serotonin reuptake inhibitors.** The SSRIs are first-line agents for the longterm management of anxiety disorders, with control gradually achieved over a 2-to 4-wk course, depending on required dosage increases. **Serotonin and norepinephrine reuptake inhibitors.** Pharmacologic agents with reuptake inhibition of serotonin and norepinephrine may be helpful in a variety of mood and anxiety disorders.

Atypical antidepressants. Antidepressants that are not FDA-approved for the treatment of a given anxiety disorder still may be beneficial for the treatment of anxiety disorders; mirtazapine acts distinctly as an alpha-2 antagonist, consequently increasing synaptic norepinephrine and serotonin, while also blocking some postsynaptic serotonergic receptors that conceptually mediate excessive anxiety when stimulated with serotonin.

Tricyclic antidepressants. Tricyclic antidepressants are a complex group of drugs that have central and peripheral anticholinergic effects, as well as sedative effects.

Benzodiazepines. Benzodiazepines often are used with antidepressants as adjunct treatment; they are especially useful in the management of acute situational anxiety disorder and adjustment disorder where the duration of pharmacotherapy is anticipated to be 6 weeks or less and for the rapid control of anxiety attacks.

Antianxiety agents. Buspirone is a non-sedating antipsychotic drug unrelated to benzodiazepines, barbiturates, and other sedative-hypnotics; it has fewer cognitive and psychomotor adverse effects, which makes its use preferable in elderly patients. **Anticonvulsant.** The drug of choice in this category is the gamma-aminobutyric acid derivative pregabalin (Lyrica).

Antihypertensive agent. Agents in this class may have a positive effect on the physiological symptoms of anxiety; beta-blockers may be useful for the circumscribed treatment of situational/performance anxiety on an as-needed basis.

Monoamine oxidase inhibitor (MAOI). MAOIs are most commonly prescribed for patients with social phobia.

Antipsychotic agent. Atypical and typical antipsychotic medications are generally used more as augmentation strategies and are second-line treatment options in generalized anxiety disorder.

Nursing Management

Nursing management of a patient with anxiety disorder includes the following:

1. Nursing Assessment

Nursing assessment of a patient with anxiety disorder includes:

History. The patient usually seeks treatment for panic disorder after he or she has experienced several panic attacks; usually, the patient cannot identify any trigger for these events.

General appearance and motor behaviour. The patient may appear entirely "normal" or may have signs of anxiety if he or she is apprehensive about having a panic attack in the next few moments.

Mood and affect. Assessment of mood and affect may reveal that the patient is anxious, worried, tense, depressed, serious, or sad.

Thought processes and content. During a panic attack, the patient is overwhelmed, believing that he or she is dying, losing control, or "going insane"; the patient may even consider suicide.

Sensorium and intellectual process. During a panic attack, the patient may be confused and disoriented; he or she cannot take in environmental cues and respond appropriately.

2. Nursing Diagnosis

Based on the assessment data, the major nursing diagnosis is:

- Anxiety related to unconscious conflict about essential values and goals of life;
- situational or maturational crises.
- Fear related to phobic stimulus.
- Ineffective coping related to underdeveloped ego; punitive superego.
- Powerlessness related to fear of disapproval from others.
- Social isolation related to panic level of anxiety.

3. Nursing Care Planning and Goals

The major nursing care planning goals for patients with Anxiety Disorders are:

The patient will verbalize ways to intervene in escalating anxiety within 1 week. The patient will be able to recognize symptoms of the onset of anxiety and intervene before reaching the panic stage by the time of discharge from treatment.

4. Nursing Interventions

The nursing interventions for anxiety disorders are:

Stay calm and be non-threatening: Maintain a calm, nonthreatening manner while working with patients; anxiety is contagious and may be transferred from staff to patient or vice versa.

Assure the patient of safety. Reassure the patient of his or her safety and security; this can be conveyed by the physical presence of the nurse; do not leave the patient alone at this time.

Be clear and concise with words: Use simple words and brief messages, and speak calmly and clearly, to explain hospital experiences to the patient; in an intensely anxious situation, the patient is unable to comprehend anything but the most elementary communication.

Provide a non-stimulating environment: Keep immediate surroundings low in stimuli (dim lighting, few people, simple decor); a stimulating environment may increase the level of anxiety.

Administer medications as prescribed: Administer tranquilizing medication, as ordered by physician; assess medication for effectiveness and for adverse side effects.

Recognize precipitating factors: When level of anxiety has been reduced, explore with patient possible reasons for occurrence; recognition of precipitating factors is the first step in teaching patient to interrupt escalation of anxiety.

Encourage patient to verbalize feelings: Encourage patient to talk about traumatic experience under nonthreatening conditions; help patient work through feelings of guilt related to the traumatic event; help patient understand that this was an event to which most people would have responded in like manner.

Evaluation

The outcome criteria for Anxiety Disorders include:

- Patient is able to maintain anxiety at level in which problem solving can be accomplished.
- Patient is able to verbalize signs and symptoms of escalating anxiety.
- Patient is able to demonstrate techniques for interrupting the progression of anxiety to the panic level.

Documentation Guidelines Documentation guidelines include the following:

- Individual findings include factors affecting, interactions, the nature of social exchanges, and specifics of individual behaviour.
- Cultural and religious beliefs, and expectations.
- Plan of Care
- Teaching plan.
- Responses to interventions, teaching, and actions performed.
- Attainment or progress toward the desired outcome.

Nursing Care Plans and Management

Nurses encounter anxious patients and families in a variety of situations. The nurse must first assess the person's anxiety level because this determines what interventions are likely to be effective. Treatment of anxiety disorders usually involves medication and therapy. A combination of both produces better results than either one alone. When working with an anxious person, the nurse must be aware of her anxiety level. It is easy for the nurse to become easily anxious – remaining calm and in control is essential if the nurse is going to work effectively with the patient.

Nursing care plans and management for patients with anxiety disorders typically include reducing anxiety levels, promoting self-care, improving coping skills, enhancing social support, and encouraging treatment compliance.

Nursing Problem Priorities

The following are the nursing priorities for patients with anxiety disorders:

- Assess anxiety levels and triggers
- Establish therapeutic rapport
- Administer prescribed anti-anxiety medication
- Monitor for signs of panic or distress
- Implement relaxation techniques and promote a calming environment
- Provide education on anxiety management
- Collaborate with the multidisciplinary team.

Nursing Assessment

Assess for the following subjective and objective data:

- Generalized Anxiety Disorder (GAD):
- Restlessness, irritability, and difficulty concentrating.
- Muscle tension, fatigue, and sleep disturbances.
- Panic Disorder:
- Rapid heart rate, chest pain, shortness of breath, and trembling/shaking.
- Fear of future panic attacks, leading to avoidance behaviours.

Social Anxiety Disorder (Social Phobia): Avoidance of social interactions, public speaking, or performing in front of others. Excessive self-consciousness, blushing, sweating, and trembling.

Specific Phobias:

Immediate anxiety response when exposed to the feared object or situation. Avoidance behaviours or extreme distress when encountering the phobic stimulus.

Obsessive-Compulsive Disorder (OCD):

Anxiety caused by obsessions and relief sought through compulsive behaviours. Examples include excessive handwashing, checking, or counting rituals.

Post-Traumatic Stress Disorder (PTSD):

Intrusive memories, flashbacks, nightmares, or distressing thoughts related to the trauma. Avoidance of reminders, emotional numbness, hypervigilance, and heightened arousal.

Nursing Diagnosis

Following a thorough assessment, a nursing diagnosis is formulated to specifically

address the challenges associated with anxiety disorders based on the nurse's

clinical judgement and understanding of the patient's unique health condition. While

nursing diagnoses serve as a framework for organizing care, their usefulness may

vary in different clinical situations. In real-life clinical settings, it is important to note

that the use of specific nursing diagnostic labels may not be as prominent or commonly utilized as other components of the care plan. It is ultimately the nurse's

clinical expertise and judgment that shape the care plan to meet the unique needs

of each patient, prioritizing their health concerns and priorities.

Nursing Goals

Goals and expected outcomes may include:

The patient will be free from injury.

The patient will discuss feelings of dread, anxiety, and so forth.

The patient will respond to relaxation techniques with a decreased anxiety level.

The patient will be able to discuss phobic objects or situations with the nurse.

The patient will be able to function in presence of a phobic object or situation without
experiencing panic anxiety by the time of discharge from treatment.

The patient will decrease participation in ritualistic behaviour.

The patient will demonstrate the ability to cope effectively.

The patient will verbalize signs and symptoms of increased anxiety and intervene to
maintain anxiety at a manageable level.

The patient will demonstrate the ability to interrupt obsessive thoughts and refrain
from ritualistic behaviours.

The patient will participate in decision-making regarding own care.

The patient will be able to effectively problem-solve ways to take control of his or
her life situation.

The patient will willingly attend therapy activities accompanied by a trusted support
person.

The patient will voluntarily spend time with other patients and staff members in group
activities.

The patient will verbalize the desire to take control of self-care activities.

The patient will be able to take care of their own ADLs and demonstrate a willingness
to do so.

The patient states correct information about medications and adverse side effects.

The patient verbalizes an understanding of the disease process, risk factors, and
therapeutic regimen.

Nursing Interventions and Actions

Therapeutic interventions and nursing actions for patients with anxiety disorders
may include:

1. Controlling and Managing Anxiety and Fear

- For high levels of anxiety are high (severe or panic); reassure the patient of his or her safety and security.

- Move the patient to a quiet area with minimal stimuli such as a small room or seclusion area (dim lighting, few people, and so on.)
- Provide reassurance and comfort measures.
- Educate the patient and/or family members that anxiety disorders are treatable.
- Support the patient's defenses initially. Maintain awareness of your feelings and level of discomfort. Use short, simple directions when the patient is in a panic attack.
- Avoid asking or forcing the patient to make choices.
- Instruct the patient that medications prescribed as needed may be indicated for high levels of anxiety. Watch out for adverse side effects.
- Encourage the patient's participation in relaxation exercises such as deep breathing, progressive muscle relaxation, guided imagery, meditation, and so forth.
- Teach signs and symptoms of escalating anxiety and ways to interrupt its progression (e.g., relaxation techniques, deep-breathing exercises, physical exercises, brisk walks, jogging, and meditation).
- Administer selective serotonin reuptake inhibitors (SSRIs) as ordered.
- Help the patient see that mild anxiety can be a positive catalyst for change and does not need to be avoided.
- Cognitive-behavioural therapy
- Exposure therapy
- Cognitive therapy
- Behavioural therapy
- Respiratory training
- Recognition of precipitating factors is the first step in teaching the patient to interrupt the escalation of anxiety.
- Reinforce information about interpersonal psychotherapy (IPT).
- Managing fear
- Determine the type of the patient's fear by thorough, rational questioning and active listening.
- Explore the patient's perception of a threat to physical integrity or a threat to self-concept.
- Present and discuss the reality of the situation with the patient to recognize aspects that can be changed and those that cannot.
- Reassure the patient of his safety and security.
- Suggest that the patient substitute positive thoughts for negative ones.

- Include the patient in making decisions related to the selection of alternative
- coping strategies.
- Encourage the patient to explore underlying feelings that may be contributing to irrational fears. Helping the patient to understand how facing these feelings, rather than suppressing them, can result in more adaptive coping abilities. Discuss the process of thinking about the feared object/situation before it occurs.
- Encourage the patient to share seemingly unnatural fears and feelings with others, especially the nurse therapist.
- Encourage to stop, wait, and not rush out of feared situations as soon as experienced. Support the use of relaxation exercises.
- Explore things that may lower fear level and keep it manageable (e.g. singing while dressing, repeating a mantra, practicing positive self-talk while in a fearful situation).
- Desensitization techniques
- Systematic desensitization
- Expose the patient to a predetermined list of anxiety-provoking stimuli rated in a hierarchy from the least frightening to the most frightening.
- Help the patient to learn how to use these techniques when confronting an actual and anxiety-provoking situation. Provide practice sessions (e.g. Roleplay) to deal with the phobic reactions in real-life situations.
- Encourage the patient to set increasingly more difficult goals.
- Administer benzodiazepines as indicated; watch out for any adverse side effects.
- Administer anti-anxiety agents as prescribed.
- Administer beta-blockers as indicated.
- Provide information about cranial electrotherapy stimulators (CES).

2. Promoting Effective Coping

- Assess the patient's ability to identify and communicate their emotions and stressors.
- Assess the patient's coping strategies and evaluate their effectiveness in managing anxiety symptoms.
- Assess the impact of the patient's personal beliefs on their ability to cope.
- Initially meet the patient's dependency needs as necessary.

- Encourage independence and give positive reinforcement for independent behaviours.
- During the beginning of treatment, allow plenty of time for rituals. Do not be judgmental or verbalize disapproval of the behaviour. Support and encourage the patient's efforts to explore the meaning and purpose of the behaviour.
- Gradually limit the amount of time allotted for ritualistic behaviour as the patient becomes more involved in unit activities.
- Encourage the recognition of situations that provoke obsessive thoughts or ritualistic behaviours.
- Provide positive reinforcement for nonritualistic behaviours.
- Avoid reinforcing maladaptive behaviours.
- Provide information about the different coping styles.
- Promote the consumption of a balanced diet and adequate hydration.
- Encourage social support, especially from family members.
- Provide referrals for support resources.
- Help identify areas of life situations that the patient can control.
- Help the patient identify areas of life situation that are not within his ability to control; encourage verbalization of these feelings.
- Note behaviours indicative of hopelessness.
- Determine the degree of life and locus of control.
- Have the patient take as much responsibility for their self-care practices.
- Help the patient set realistic goals.
- Identify ways and instances in which the patient can achieve and encourage participation in these activities; provide positive reinforcement for participation.
- Incorporate the patient's daily routine into the home care schedule or hospital stay, as possible.
- Discuss needs openly and facilitate actions to meet identified needs.
- Discuss plans for the future and include family members in the planning.
- Identify the extent of social isolation.
- Assess for signs of depression.
- Convey an accepting and positive attitude by making brief, frequent contacts.
- Show unconditional positive regard.
- Be honest, and empathetic and keep all promises.
- Be cautious with touch. Allow the patient extra space and an avenue for exit if he becomes too anxious.

- Administer tranquilizing medications as ordered; monitor adverse side effects.
- Discuss with the patient the signs of increasing anxiety and techniques for
- interrupting the response such as breathing exercises, thought-stopping, relaxation, and meditation.
- Give recognition and positive reinforcement for the patient's voluntary interaction with others.
- Provide referrals to support groups and community resources.
- Reinforce information about psychotherapy.

3. Assisting in Self-Care

- Keep strict records of food and fluid intake.
- Assess the patient's ability to self-manage.
- Urge the patient to perform normal ADLs to his level of ability.
- Encourage independence. Intervene when the patient is unable to perform.
- Offer recognition and positive reinforcement for independent accomplishments.
- Show the patient how to perform activities with which he is having difficulty.
- Offer nutritious snacks and fluids between meals.
- Promote exercise and physical activities.
- Assist patients in choosing self-care activities that they can perform within their abilities.

4. Initiating Patient Education and Health Teachings

- Assess for nausea, headache, nervousness, insomnia, agitation, and sexual dysfunction.
- Assess for fatigue, drowsiness, and cognitive impairments.
- Assess the patient's and family members' understanding of anxiety disorders.
- Assess for possible barriers to learning about and accepting treatment for anxiety disorders.

- Utilize psychometric tools in assessing the patient's experiences about stress and other mental health-related factors.
- Explain the physiologic action of SSRI in relieving anxiety.
- Reinforce that a gradual tapering is necessary when a benzodiazepine is discontinued.
- Encourage the patient and family members to engage in educational programs about mental health.
- Promote smoking cessation and decreased alcohol intake.
- Provide information about self-help guides for mental health concerns.
- Refer to reliable internet sources for educational purposes.
- Monitor the effects of benzodiazepines among older adult patients with anxiety disorders.
- Emphasize the importance of follow-up consultations.
- Encourage family members to ask questions.
- Evaluate the effects of maintenance treatment and relay to the patient and their families.

5. Administer Medications and Provide Pharmacologic Support

Selective serotonin reuptake inhibitors (SSRIs): These medications work by increasing serotonin levels, a neurotransmitter involved in regulating mood, in the brain.

- Escitalopram (Lexapro): Given for the treatment of generalized anxiety disorder (GAD) and social anxiety disorder.
- Sertraline (Zoloft): Effective in treating various anxiety disorders, including panic disorder, social anxiety disorder, post-traumatic stress disorder (PTSD), and obsessive-compulsive disorder (OCD).
- Fluoxetine (Prozac): Approved for panic disorder, OCD, and bulimia nervosa. It is also used off-label for social anxiety disorder.
- Paroxetine (Paxil): Used to treat various anxiety disorders, including panic disorder, GAD, social anxiety disorder, and PTSD.
- Citalopram (Celexa): Primarily used for depression but also prescribed off-label for anxiety disorders, such as panic disorder, GAD, and social anxiety disorder.

Benzodiazepines

Biological factors may be involved in phobic/panic reactions, and these

medications (particularly Xanax) produce a rapid calming effect and may help the patient change behaviour by keeping anxiety low during learning and desensitization sessions. The risk of addiction to benzodiazepines should be carefully considered before use in anxiety disorders. Benzodiazepines should not be used in patients with a prior
history of alcohol or other drug abuse.

Anxiolytics

Buspirone is a nonsedating antipsychotic drug unrelated to benzodiazepines, barbiturates, and other sedative-hypnotics. This is a novel antianxiety agent that is comparable with benzodiazepines in reducing symptoms of anxiety. Buspirone also has fewer cognitive and psychomotor adverse effects, which makes it preferable in older adults. Major limitations include a lack of anti-panic activity and reduced anxiolytic effects in patients recently withdrawn from benzodiazepines.

Beta-blockers

Beta-blockers control the physical symptoms of anxiety such as rapid heart rate, a trembling voice, sweating, dizziness, and shaky hands. They are most helpful for phobias, particularly social phobias.

CHAPTER VIII

PSYCHIATRIC NURSING IN MAJOR DEPRESSION

As per the Diagnostic and Statistical Manual of Mental Disorders, 5th Edition (DSM-5), an individual must have five (5) of the following symptoms, of which one must be a depressed mood or anhedonia causing social or occupational impairment, to be diagnosed with major depressive disorder (MDD):

- Persistently low or depressed mood
- Anhedonia or decreased interest in pleasurable activities
- Feelings of guilt or worthlessness
- Lack of energy
- Poor concentration
- Appetite changes
- Psychomotor retardation or agitation
- Sleep disturbances
- Suicidal thoughts

The DSM-5 also classifies depressive disorders as:

- Disruptive mood dysregulation disorder
- Major depressive disorder
- Persistent depressive disorder (dysthymia)
- Premenstrual dysphoric disorder
- Depressive disorder due to another medical condition

Furthermore, depressive disorders may be further categorized by **specifiers:**

- Peripartum onset
- Seasonal pattern
- Melancholic features
- Mood-congruent or mood-incongruent psychotic features
- Anxious distress
- Catatonia

Major depressive disorder is a clinical diagnosis; it is mainly diagnosed by the clinical history given by the patient and mental status examination. The clinical interview must include medical history, family history, social history, and substance abuse history along with symptomatology. A complete physical examination, including a neurological examination, should also be performed.

Nursing Care Plans and Management

Nursing care plans and management for patients with major depression include:

1. Determining a degree of impairment,
2. Assessing the patient's coping abilities
3. Assisting the patient to deal with the current situation,
4. Increasing the patient's self-esteem
5. Promoting the patient's safety
6. Improving the patient's social support, and
7. Promoting health and wellness.

Nursing Problem Priorities

The following are the nursing priorities for patients with major depression:

- *Assess suicide risk*
- *Monitor mood and behaviour changes*
- *Administer prescribed antidepressant medication*
- *Facilitate regular psychotherapy sessions*
- *Provide education on depression management*
- *Nursing Assessment*
- *Assess for the following subjective and objective data:*
- *Persistent feelings of sadness, emptiness, or hopelessness*
- *Loss of interest or pleasure in activities once enjoyed (anhedonia)*
- *Significant changes in appetite or weight (either loss or gain)*
- *Insomnia or excessive sleepiness (hypersomnia)*
- *Fatigue or loss of energy*
- *Feelings of worthlessness or excessive guilt*
- *Difficulty concentrating or making decisions*
- *Restlessness or slowed movements*
- *Recurrent thoughts of death or suicide*
- *Social withdrawal or isolation*

Nursing Diagnosis

Following a thorough assessment, a nursing diagnosis is formulated to specifically address the challenges associated with major depression based on the nurse's clinical judgment and understanding of the patient's unique health condition. While nursing diagnoses serve as a framework for organizing care, their usefulness may vary in different clinical situations. In real-life clinical settings, it is important to note

that the use of specific nursing diagnostic labels may not be as prominent or commonly utilized as other components of the care plan. It is ultimately the nurse's clinical expertise and judgment that shape the care plan to meet the unique needs of each patient, prioritizing their health concerns and priorities.

Nursing Goals

Goals and expected outcomes may include:

The patient will seek help when experiencing self-destructive impulses.

The patient will have a behavioural manifestation of absent depression.

The patient will identify at least two-three people he/she can seek out for support and emotional guidance when he/she is feeling self-destructive before discharge.

The patient will not inflict any harm to themself or others.

The patient will identify support and support groups with whom he/she is in contact within one month.

The patient will state that he/she wants to live.

The patient will start working on constructive plans for the future. The patient will demonstrate compliance with any medication or treatment plan within the next two weeks.

The patient will identify feelings that lead to poor social interactions.

The patient will discuss two-three alternative ways to take when feeling the need to withdraw.

The patient will eventually voluntarily attend individual/group therapeutic meetings within a therapeutic milieu (community or hospital).

The patient will verbalize that he/she enjoys interacting with others in activities and one-on-one interactions to the extent they did before becoming depressed.

The patient will state and demonstrate progress in the resumption of sustaining relationships with friends and family members within one month.

The patient will feel connected with others to share thoughts, feelings, and beliefs.

The patient will feel connectedness with the inner self.

The patient will participate in spiritual rites and passages.

The patient will discuss with the nurse two things that gave his or her life meaning in the past within three days.

The patient will talk to a nurse or a spiritual leader about spiritual conflicts and concerns within three days.

The patient will keep a journal tracking thoughts and feelings for one week.

The patient will state that he/she feels a sense of forgiveness.

The patient will state that he/she wants to participate in former creative activities.

The patient will state that he/she gained comfort from previous spiritual practices.

The patient will demonstrate a zest for life and the ability to enjoy the present.

The patient will identify one or two strengths by the end of the day.

The patient will identify two unrealistic self-expectations and reformulate more realistic life goals with the nurse by the end of the day.

The patient will identify three judgemental terms (e.g., "I am lazy") the patient uses to describe themself and identify objective terms to replace them (e.g., " I do not feel motivated to).

The patient will keep a daily load and identify on a scale of 1 to 10 (1 being the lowest, 10 being the highest) feelings of guilt, shame, and self-hate.

The patient will report decreased feelings of guilt, shame, and self-hate by using a scale of 1 to 10 (1 being the lowest, 10 being the highest).

The patient will demonstrate the ability to modify unrealistic self-expectations.

The patient will give an accurate and nonjudgmental account of four positive qualities as well as identify two areas he or she wishes to improve.

The patient will identify two goals he or she wants to achieve from treatment, with aid of nursing intervention, within one to two days.

The patient will discuss with the nurse two irrational thoughts about self and others by the end of the first day.

The patient will reframe three irrational thoughts with the nurse.

The patient will remember to keep appointments, attend activities, and attend to grooming with minimal reminders from others within one to three weeks.

The patient will identify negative thoughts and rationally counter them and/or reframe them in a positive manner within two weeks.

The patient will show improved mood as demonstrated by the Beck Depression Inventory.

The patient will give examples showing that short-term memory and concentration have improved to usual levels.

The patient will demonstrate an increased ability to make appropriate decisions when planning with the nurse.

The patient will groom and dress appropriately with help from nursing staff and/ or family.

The patient will regain a more normal elimination pattern with the aid of foods high in roughage, increased fluid intake, and exercise daily (also with the aid of medications).

The patient will sleep between four to six hours with the aid of nursing measures and/or medications.

The patient will gain one pound a week with encouragement from family, significant others, and/or staff if significant weight loss is noted.

The patient will demonstrate progress in the maintenance of adequate hygiene and be appropriately groomed and dressed (shave/makeup, clothes clean and neat).

The patient will experience normal elimination with the aid of diet, fluids, and exercise within three weeks.

The patient will sleep between six to eight hours per night within one month.

The patient will gradually return to weight consistent for height and age or baseline before the illness.

The patient will engage in self-care activities at his or her own pace.

The patient will demonstrate improvement in handling the stages of grief at his or her own pace.

The patient will verbalize a sense of improvement toward the resolution of hope and grief in the subsequent time.

The patient will express feelings and acceptance of life events over which he or she has no control.

The patient will demonstrate independent problem-solving techniques to take control over life and does not verbalize or demonstrate suicidality. The patient and significant other will verbalize accurate information about at least two of the possible causes of depression, three to four of the signs and symptoms of depression, and the use of medications, psychotherapy, and electroconvulsive therapy as treatment.

Nursing Interventions and Actions

1.Mental Health Diagnosis and Therapeutic interventions

These interventions and nursing actions for patients with major depression may include:

- Assist in establishing a safety plan.
- Activate links to self-help groups.
- Perform post-discharge follow-up interventions.
- Prepare the patient for electroconvulsive therapy (ECT) as indicated.
- Provide close monitoring for paediatric patients taking antidepressants.
- Remove anything that the patient may use to hurt or kill themselves.
- Administer antidepressants, as prescribed.
- Assess individual signs of hopelessness.
- Assess destructive behaviours used to handle feelings such as withdrawal, avoidance, and substance abuse.
- Conduct a suicide assessment to identify the level of suicide risk.
- Determine the degree of life mastery and locus control.
- Allow the patient to express feelings and perceptions
- Express hope to the patient with realistic comments about the patient's strengths and resources.
- Assist the patient in determining aspects of life that are under his or her control.
- Allow the patient to assume responsibility for self-care, such as setting realistic goals, scheduling activities, and making independent decisions.
- Aid the patient to determine aspects of life events that are not within his or her ability to control. Discuss feelings related to this lack of control.
- Encourage the patient to examine spiritual supports that may provide hope.
- Educate the patient about crisis intervention services such as suicide hotlines and other resources.
- Administer antidepressants as indicated.
- Identify community resources, such as the adult day enrichment program.
- Discuss with the patient their expectations for themselves, their family, the community, and healthcare workers.

2. Promoting Therapeutic Relationship and Enhancing Support Network

- Assess the patient using depression screening tests.
- Depression screening tests can be valuable, with the most widely used one being the Patient Health Questionnaire-9 (PHQ-9). However, it is important to understand that the results obtained from the use of any depression screening or rating scales do not diagnose depression and may be imperfect in any population, especially in older adults. The simplest screening test is a single question: Are you depressed?
- The PHQ-9 is a 9-item depression scale; each item is scored 0 to 3, providing a 0 to 27 severity score.
- Review family patterns of relating and social behaviours.
- Initially, provide activities that require minimal concentration (e.g., drawing, playing simple board games).
- Involve the patient in gross motor activities that call for very little concentration (e.g., walking).
- When the patient is in the most depressed state, involve the patient in one-to-one activity.
- Eventually maximize the patient's contacts with others (first one other, then two others, etc.).
- Refer the patient and family to self-help groups in the community.
- Prepare the patient for cognitive behavioural therapy (CBT).
- Encourage the patient to express feelings and perceptions of problems.
- Discuss negative self-concepts and self-talk.
- Ensure that the patient has a solid support system once discharged.
- Assess what spiritual practices have offered comfort and meaning to the patient's life when not ill.
- Assess whether the patient is experiencing spiritual struggles or difficulties.
- Encourage the patient to write a journal expressing thoughts and reflections daily. The written essays offer rich information to track mechanisms of therapeutic change.
- If the patient is unable to write, provide a tape recorder.
- Discuss with the patient what has given comfort and meaning to the person in the past.
- Suggest that the spiritual leader affiliated with the facility contact the patient.
- Provide information on referrals, when needed, for religious or spiritual information (e.g., readings, programs, tapes, and community resources).
- Listen to the patient's reports and expressions of anger or concern.

- Explore ways that spirituality or religious practices, such as music, prayer,
- meditation, and rituals have affected the patient's life.
- Use therapeutic communication skills of gentle stillness, reflection, conveying respect through tone of voice and body language, and active listening.
- Review coping skills used and their effectiveness in the current situation.

3. Promoting Activities of Daily Living and Self-Care

- Determine the patient's previous level of cognitive functioning (from the patient, family, and past medical records).
- Use measures to assess cognitive functioning.
- Assess the patient's cognition using measures that reflect real-world function.
- Determine factors that may affect the patient's cognitive function.
- Use simple, concrete words.
- Allow the patient to have plenty of time to think and frame responses.
- Allow more time than usual for the patient to finish usual activities of daily living (ADL) (e.g., eating, dressing).
- Help the patient to postpone important major life decision-making.
- While the patient is severely depressed, minimize the patient's responsibility.
- Help the patient identify negative thinking/thoughts. Teach the patient to reframe and/or refute negative thoughts.
- Help the patient and family structure an environment that can help re-establish set schedules and predictable routines during severe depression.
- Administer tricyclic antidepressants (TCAs): as prescribed.
- Administer mood stabilizers as indicated.
- Reinforce information regarding cognitive remediation.
- Encourage the patient to engage in regular physical exercise.
- Determine the usual level of functioning using the Functional Level Classification 0 to 4 for status.
- Assess barriers to participation in self-care.
- Assisting in bathing or hygiene
- Encourage the use of soap, washcloths, toothbrushes, shaving equipment, makeup, etc.

- Give step-by-step reminders such as "Brush the teeth "Clean the outer surfaces of your upper teeth, then your lower teeth. . ."
- Managing constipation and effective bowel movement
- Monitor intake and output, especially bowel movements.
- Encourage the intake of non-alcoholic and noncaffeinated fluids, six to eight glasses daily.
- Offer fibre-rich foods and periods of exercise.
- Evaluate the need for laxatives and enemas.
- Promoting adequate sleep
- Provide rest periods after activities or engage in relaxation activities.
- Encourage relaxation measures in the evening (e.g., drinking warm milk, a back rub, or a tepid bath).
- Encourage the patient to get up and dress and to stay out of bed during the day.
- Reduce environmental and physical stimulants in the evening; provide decaffeinated coffee, soft music, soft lights, and quiet activities.
- Promoting adequate nutrition
- Weigh the patient weekly and observe the eating patterns of the patient.
- Encourage eating with others.
- Serve foods or drinks the patient likes.
- Encourage small, high-calorie, and high-protein snacks and fluids frequently throughout the day and evening if weight loss is noted.
- Allow the patient sufficient time to accomplish tasks. Maintain a supportive but firm attitude.
- Provide positive feedback for efforts and accomplishments.
- Avoid doing things for the patient when they can do them for themselves. Provide assistance only when necessary.

4. Providing Emotional Support and Enhancing Self-Esteem

- Assess the self-esteem level of the patient.
- Assess the dynamics of the patient and family members, including the patient's role in the family and cultural factors.
- Allow the patient to perform personal care activities.
- Give positive feedback after a task is achieved.
- Allow the patient to engage in simple recreational activities, advancing to more complex activities in a group environment.

- Teach visualization techniques that can help the patient replace negative selfimages with more positive images and thoughts.
- Encourage the patient to participate in group therapy where the members share the same situations/feelings that they have.
- Evaluate the patient's need for assertiveness training tools to pursue things he or she wants or needs in life. Arrange for training through community-based programs, personal counselling, literature, etc.
- Involve the patient in activities that he or she wants to improve by using problemsolving skils.
- Assess and evaluate the need for more teaching in this area.
- Work with the patient to identify cognitive distortions that encourage negative selfappraisal.
- For example:
- Discounting positive attributes
- Mind reading
- Overgeneralizations
- Self-blame
- Help the patient become aware of their cognitive distortions.
- Focus on negative qualities.
- Assuming others "do not like me". for example, without any real evidence that assumptions are correct.
- Taking one fact or event and making a general rule out of it. ("He always", I never").
- Consistent self-blame for everything perceived as negative.
- Encourage the patient to utilize optimism in daily life.
- Prepare the patient for mindfulness-based cognitive therapy (MBCT).
- Ask the patient about the losses that happen in his or her life. Discuss how the patient views them.
- Assess the patient's religious beliefs and cultural practices in terms of how they handled their previous losses.
- Allow the patient to recognize and express feelings and determine the connection between the feelings and the event.
- Suggest alternative methods to determine and cope with underlying feelings of anger, hurt, and rejection.
- If indicated, mention stories of how others have dealt with the same experience.
- Discuss and educate the patient on the normal stages of grief and accept the reality of related feelings such as guilt, anger, and powerlessness.

- Assist the patient in determining the problem, recognizing the need to address the problem differently, and thoroughly describing all facets of the problem.
- Assist the patient in recognizing early signs of depression and identify methods to mitigate these signs. If the symptoms persist or worsen, suggest other professional support.
- Encourage the patient's family and friends for social support.
- Promote the resumption of activities of daily living as soon as possible.
- Refer to other resources for counselling, spiritual, or pastoral care, and psychotherapy, as indicated.

5. Initiating Patient Education and Health Teachings

- Assess the patient's and significant other's knowledge regarding depression and its causes.
- Identify barriers to seeking knowledge and treatment of depression.
- Assess the level of the patient's and family members' health literacy.
- Assess the level of awareness about the stigma of mental illnesses.
- Determine the patient's and family member's level of education.
- Explain to the patient and significant others the major symptoms of depression.
- Inform the patient and significant others that depression can be treated through medications and psychotherapy.
- Discuss the purpose of electroconvulsive therapy (ECT) if indicated.
- Reinforce the importance of medication and treatment adherence.
- Include the family members or caregivers in the development of a treatment plan.
- Provide additional information about treatment-resistant depression.
- Fully disclose to the parents of paediatric patients the implications of
- pharmacotherapy and psychotherapy, as well as their responsibilities upon commencement of these therapies.
- Counsel pregnant women regarding approved therapies for them.
- Inform the patient and family members about diet restrictions when taking monoamine oxidase inhibitors (MAOIs).

6. Administer Medications and Provide Pharmacologic Support
Antidepressants
Selective serotonin reuptake inhibitors (SSRIs) have the advantage of ease

of dosing and low toxicity in overdose. SSRIs are greatly preferred over the other classes of antidepressants for the treatment of children and adolescents, and they are also the first-line medications for late-onset depression. The adverse-effect

profile of SSRIs is less prominent than that of some other agents, which promotes better adherence.

Selective serotonin reuptake inhibitors (SSRIs) such as escitalopram, sertraline, fluoxetine, and paroxetine.

SSRIs work by increasing the levels of serotonin in the brain, which helps improve mood.

Serotonin-norepinephrine reuptake inhibitors (SNRIs) such as venlafaxine and duloxetine.

SNRIs work by increasing the levels of serotonin and norepinephrine, two neurotransmitters associated with mood regulation.

Tricyclic antidepressants (TCAs) such as amitriptyline and nortriptyline TCAs work by increasing the levels of serotonin and norepinephrine in the brain.

Monoamine oxidase inhibitors (MAOIs) such as phenelzine and tranylcypromine MAOIs work by inhibiting the enzyme monoamine oxidase, which helps regulate the levels of neurotransmitters in the brain.

Atypical antidepressants such as bupropion and mirtazapine Atypical antidepressants work through various mechanisms to modulate neurotransmitter levels and improve mood.

CHAPTER IX

PSYCHIATRIC NURSING IN SUICIDAL PATIENT

Nursing Interventions and Actions

1. Risk assessment and establishing therapeutic relationship
2. Establishing safety measures
3. Providing crisis intervention
4. Emotional support and building self-esteem
5. Promoting positive coping mechanisms
6. Managing hopelessness

1.Nursing Risk Assessment and establishing therapeutic relationship

Nurse must assess for the following subjective and objective data:

- *History of prior suicide attempt*
- *Expressing active Suicidal ideation or behaviour*
- *Severe depression, delusions, or hallucinations*
- *Substance abuse or withdrawal*
- *Hopelessness, despair, increased anxiety*
- *Poor judgment, Hopelessness/helplessness*
- *Unable to cope, problem solving of stressors*
- *Denying treatment, not seeking help*
- *Avoiding food, and basic life support*
- *Not showing interest in healthcare*
- *Passivity, decreased verbalization*
- *Turning away from the speaker*

Assess for factors related to the cause of suicidal ideation: Alcohol and substance abuse/use

- *Childhood abuse*
- *Family history of suicide*
- *Grief, bereavement/loss of an important relationship*
- *Legal or disciplinary problems*
- *Physical illness, chronic pain, terminal illness*
- *Psychiatric illness (e.g., bipolar disorder, depression, schizophrenia)*
- *Poor support system, loneliness*
- *Inadequate resources and opportunity to prepare for a stressor*
- *Personal loss, unemployment, or threat of rejection*
- *Conflictual interpersonal relationships*

Basic principles of Nursing in Suicidal patient

1.Establish a Therapeutic Relationship

2.Conduct a Comprehensive Assessment.

3.Implement Safety Measures. Take immediate steps to ensure the patient's safety.

4.Collaborate on a Safety Plan. Work collaboratively with the patient to develop a personalized safety plan that includes strategies to manage suicidal thoughts or urges.

5.Provide Education and Support. Educate the patient and their family about suicide risk factors, warning signs, and available resources.

2. Establishing safety measures

- Arrange for the patient to stay with family or friends. A hospitalization is considered if there is no one available especially if the person is highly suicidal.
- Encourage the patient to avoid decisions during the time of crisis until alternatives can be considered.
- Encourage the patient to talk freely about feelings and help plan alternative ways of handling disappointment, anger, and frustration.
- Weapons and pills are removed by friends, relatives, or the nurse.
- If anxiety is extremely high, or the patient has not slept in days, a tranquilizer might be prescribed. Only a one to three-day supply of medication should be given.
- A family member or significant other should monitor pills for safety.
- Contact family members, and arrange for individual and/ or family crisis counselling. Activate links to self-help groups.
- Provide information about technological advances that can be used to reduce suicidality.

3. Providing crisis intervention

- During the crisis period, healthcare workers will continue to emphasize the following four points: the crisis is temporary, unbearable pain can be survived, help is available, and you are not alone.
- Prepare the patient for electroconvulsive therapy (ECT).
- Follow unit protocol for suicide regarding creating a safe environment (taking away potential weapons– belts, sharp objects, items, and so on).

- Keep accurate and thorough records of the patient's behaviours (verbal and physical) and all nursing/physician actions.
- Put on either suicide precaution (one-on-one monitoring at one arm's length away) or suicide observation (15-minute visual check of mood, behaviour, and verbatim statements), depending on the level of suicide potential.
- Keep accurate and timely records, and document the patient's activity, usually every 15 minutes (what the patient is doing, with whom, and so on). Follow unit protocol.
- Encourage the patient to talk about their feelings and problem-solve alternatives.
- Construct a no-suicide contract or a crisis safety plan.

4. Emotional support and building self-esteem

- Assess for feelings of apathy, hopelessness, and depression.
- Determine the patient's power needs or need for control.
- Distinguish the patient's locus of control.
- Evaluate the patient's decision-making competence.
- Know situations/interactions that may add to the patient's sense of powerlessness.
- Assess the role of illness plays in the patient's sense of powerlessness.
- Note if the patient shows a need for information about illness, treatment plan, and procedures.
- Evaluate the results of the information given on the patient's feelings and behaviour.
- Encourage verbalization of feelings, thoughts, and concerns about making decisions.
- Encourage the patient to identify strengths.
- This will aid the patient to recognize inner strengths.
- Appraise the impact of powerlessness on the patient's physical condition (e.g., appearance, oral intake, hygiene, sleep habits).
- Discuss with the patient concerning his or her care (e.g., treatment options, the convenience of visits, or the time of ADLs).
- Encourage an increased responsibility for self.
- Help the patient reexamine negative perceptions of the situation. Eliminate the unpredictability of events by allowing adequate preparation for tests or procedures.

- Give the patient control over their environment.
- This approach enhances the patient's independence.
- Aid the patient in recognizing the importance of culture, religion, race, gender, and age on his or her sense of powerlessness.
- Support in planning and creating a timetable to manage increased responsibility in the future.
- Avoid using coercive power when approaching the patient.
- Render positive feedback for making decisions and engaging in self-care.

5. Promoting positive coping mechanisms

- Assess the patient's strengths and positive coping skills (talking to others, creative outlets, social activities, problem-solving abilities).
- Assess the patient's coping behaviours that are not effective and that result in negative sequelae: angry outbursts, denial, drinking, procrastination, and withdrawal.
- Assess the need for assertiveness training. Assertiveness skills can help the patient develop a sense of balance and control.
- Assess the patient's social support.
- Identify situations that trigger suicidal thoughts.
- Assess for the presence of defining characteristics.
- Assess for the influence of cultural beliefs, norms, and values on the patient's perceptions of effective coping.
- Observe for causes of ineffective coping such as poor self-concept, grief, lack of problem-solving skills, lack of support, or recent change in life situation.
- Assess for intergenerational family problems that can overwhelm coping abilities.
- Identify specific stressors.
- Observe for strengths such as the ability to relate the facts and to acknowledge the source of stressors.
- Determine the patient's understanding of the stressful situation.
- Analyse past use of coping mechanisms including decision-making and problem-solving.
- Monitor the risk of harming self or others and intervene appropriately.
- Evaluate resources and support systems available to the patient.
- Clarify those things that are not under the person's control. One cannot control others actions, likes, choices, or health status.

- Encouraging the patient to express feelings and emotions, actively listening, and providing support and empathy.
- Assist the patient in identifying and addressing negative thoughts and cognitive distortions.
- Encourage the patient to participate in activities that promote a sense of purpose and accomplishment, such as exercising, learning a new skill, volunteering, or attending workshops/classes.
- Promote the use of several coping strategies as determined by the patient.
- Prepare the patient for psychotherapy, such as interpersonal psychotherapy.
- Provide information about the types of coping styles.
- Set a working relationship with the patient through continuity of care.
- Assist patients set realistic goals and identify personal skills and knowledge.
- Provide chances to express concerns, fears, feelings, and expectations.
- Use empathetic communication.
- Convey feelings of acceptance and understanding. Avoid false reassurances.
- Encourage the patient to make choices and participate in the planning of care and scheduled activities.
- Encourage the patient to recognize their own strengths and abilities.
- Consider mental and physical activities within the patient's ability (e.g., reading, television, outings, movies, radio, crafts, exercise, sports, games, dinners out, and social gatherings).
- Assist patients with accurately evaluating the situation and their own accomplishments.
- If the patient is physically capable, encourage moderate aerobic exercise.
- Provide information about the patient's wants and needs. Do not give more than the patient can handle.
- Provide touch therapy with permission. Give the patient a back massage using slow, rhythmic stroking with hands. Use a rate of 60 strokes a minute for 3 minutes on 2-inch-wide areas on both sides of the spinous process from the crown to the sacral area.
- Assist the patient with problem-solving in a constructive manner.
- Provide information and explanation regarding care before care is given.
- Eliminate stimuli in an environment that could be misinterpreted as threatening.

- Discuss changes with patients before making them.
- Provide outlets that foster feelings of personal achievement and self-esteem.
- Point out signs of positive progress or change.
- Encourage the use of cognitive behavioural relaxation (e.g., music therapy, guided imagery).
- Be supportive of coping behaviours; give the patient time to relax.
- Discuss with the patient his or her previous stressors and the coping mechanisms used.
- Use distraction techniques during procedures that cause patient to be fearful.
- Apply systematic desensitization when introducing new people, places, or procedures that may cause fear and altered coping.
- Refer for counselling as necessary.
- Evaluate for suicidal tendencies. Refer for mental health care immediately if indicated.
- Refer to medical social services for evaluation and counselling.
- If the patient is associated with the mental health system, actively engage in mental health team planning.

6. Managing hopelessness

- Assess the patient's emotional state, including symptoms of depression, anxiety, and hopelessness.
- Assess the patient's level of social support, including relationships with family and friends.
- Assess physical appearances such as grooming, posture, and hygiene.
- Ascertain the role that illness presents in the patient's hopelessness.
- Assess the patient's understanding of the situation, belief in self, and his or her own abilities.
- Assess the patient for and point out reasons for living.
- Assess the patient's willingness to eat, sleeping patterns, and daily activities.
- Evaluate the patient's ability to establish goals, make decisions, and solve problems.
- Determine the patient's social support system and possible source of hope.
- Ascertain the patient's expectations for the future.

- Encourage patients to look into their negative thinking, and reframe negative thinking into neutral objective thinking.
- Work with the patient to identify areas of strength.
- Point out unrealistic and perfectionistic thinking.
- Identify things that have given meaning and joy to live in the past. Discuss how these things can be reincorporated into their present lifestyle (e.g., religious or
- spiritual beliefs, group activities, creative endeavours).
- Spend time discussing the patient's dreams and wishes for the future. Identify short-term goals they can set for the future.
- Encourage contact with religious or spiritual persons or groups that have supplied comfort and support in the patient's past.
- Teach the patient steps in the problem-solving process.
- Encourage the patient to utilize effective coping styles.
- Develop a trusting relationship with the patient.
- Take time to listen to verbalization of hopelessness, suicidal thoughts, and lack of self-worth.
- Acknowledge acceptance of the expression of feelings: Active listening may help patients express themselves.
- Learn whether the patient perceives unachieved outcomes as failures or emphasizes failures instead of accomplishments.
- Encourage a positive mental perspective, discourage negative thoughts, and brace patient for negative results.
- Provide openings for the patient to verbalize feelings of hopelessness.
- The nurse promotes a supportive environment by taking time to listen to the patient in a nonjudgemental way.
- Manage to have consistency in staff appointed to care for the patient.
- Identify previous coping strategies and their effectiveness.
- Assist the patient with looking at options and establishing goals that are relevant to him or her.
- Encourage the patient to recognize his or her own strengths and abilities.
- Promoting awareness can facilitate the use of these strengths.
- Work with the patient to set small, attainable goals.
- Render physical care that the patient is unable to achieve and respect the patient's abilities.
- Stay and spend time with the patient. Use empathy; try to understand what the patient is saying, and communicate this understanding to the patient.

- Assist the patient in establishing realistic goals by recognizing short-term goals and revising them as needed.
- Help the patient in developing a realistic appraisal of the situation.
- Promote an attitude of realistic hope.
- Send feelings of acceptance and understanding. Avoid false reassurances.
- Provide time for the patient to initiate interactions.
- Strengthen the patient's relationship with significant others; allow them to take part in the patient's care.
- Encourage family and significant others to display care, hope, and love for the patient.
- Practice touch, if appropriate and with authority, to show care, and encourage the family to do the same.
- Present opportunities for the patient to manage the care setting.
- Promote the use of spiritual resources as desired.
- Provide plant or pet therapy if possible.
- Refer the patient to self-help groups such as I Can Cope and Make Today Count.

CHAPTER X

PSYCHIATRIC NURSING IN ACUTE CONFUSION/ DELIRIUM AND ALTERED MENTAL STATUS

The term 'confusion' can range from dullness to delirium. It is a symptom of cerebral or brain metabolism due to various reasons. Onset of confusion can range from acute to chronic. Fluctuating course is very common.

The predominant symptoms of acute confusional state or delirium includes

1. Altered arousal levels: Patient may not respond to verbal commands easily and may need pain/pressure stimulus to be woken up (hypoactive delirium) 'or' patient may be screaming actively (hyperactive delirium)

2. Disorientation to time, place and person: The patient usually loses touch with his surroundings due to disturbance of sleep and wakefulness. Wandering away from home, not able to identify his bed in hospital, being lost is common.

3. Reversal of sleep wake cycle: Patient will be actively awake as the sun sets (sundowning) and whole night, and may sleep in the day. This is due to altered circadian rhythm.

4. Changes in cognitive functions: Immediate, recent memory may be affected. Assessment can be difficult depending on level of cooperation.

5. Psychotic symptoms: Delusion of persecution can cause fearfulness and patient will not allow any clinical procedure to be done. Visual hallucinations are very common and patient will pull out intravenous, urinary catheters. Unintentional harm and falls are common.

6. Mood changes: Patient may be very irritable mostly due to loss of touch with environmental stimuli.

Nursing assessment

A careful and complete physical examination including a mental status examination is necessary. Testing vital signs such as temperature, pulse, blood pressure, and respiration is mandatory. Healthcare providers depend on nursing notes or health records for identifying a fluctuating course, therefore, documentation of the signs and symptoms observed is essential.

Goals and outcomes

- The nursing goals and outcomes for acute confusion aim to identify and treat the underlying cause of confusion, promote safety and prevent harm, optimize patient cognition and functional status, and educate patients and families about strategies to manage acute confusion.
- The patient has diminished episodes of delirium.
- The patient regains normal reality orientation and level of consciousness.
- The patient verbalizes understanding of causative factors when known.
- The patient initiates lifestyle/behaviour changes to prevent or minimize the recurrence of the problem.
- The patient demonstrates appropriate motor behaviour.
- The patient participates in activities of daily living (ADLs).

Nursing assessment and rationales

Nursing care plan: The nursing assessment for acute confusion involves gathering information on the patient's cognitive function, medical history, medication use, and potential contributing factors to identify the underlying cause of confusion and develop an effective care plan.

1. Identify factors present, including substance abuse, seizure history, recent ECT therapy, episodes of fever/pain, presence of acute infection (especially urinary tract infection in older adult patients), exposure to toxic substances, traumatic events; change in environment, including unfamiliar noises, excessive visitors. These baseline pieces of information assist in developing a specific plan. Almost any medical illness, intoxication, or medication can cause delirium or acute confusion. Often, it is multifactorial in aetiology, therefore, each cause contributing to it must be assessed. Other causes may include postictal state and unfamiliar environments.

2. Conduct an accurate mental status exam using available and reliable assessment tools. The Confusion Assessment Method for the ICU (CAM-ICU) and the Intensive Care Delirium Screening Checklist (ICDSC) are two of the validated delirium screening tools for the intensive care unit. The CAM-ICU is the most reliable score for detecting delirium in the ICU. In addition to the Nursing Delirium Screening Scale (Nu-DESC), the 3D-CAM is a validated measurement tool for the general medical unit.

3. Assess the patient's behaviour and cognition systematically and continually throughout the day and night as appropriate. Delirium always involves an acute change in mental status; therefore, knowledge of the patient's baseline mental status is key in assessing delirium. Disturbance of the sleep-wake cycle with

insomnia, daytime drowsiness, or disturbing dreams and nightmares can occur. Patients are often unable to remember why they are in the hospital or the events that occurred during the delirious period.

4. Evaluate and report possible physiological changes (e.g., sepsis, hypoglycaemia, hypotension, infection, changes in temperature, fluid and electrolyte imbalances, medications with known cognitive and psychotropic side effects). Such changes may be contributing to confusion and must be corrected. When diagnosing delirium or acute confusion, it is essential to establish that the disorder is not due to other

neurocognitive causes and that it cannot be explained by the pathophysiological effects of the physical disease.

5. Closely monitor lab results. Monitor laboratory values, noting hypoxemia, electrolyte imbalances, BUN, creatinine, ammonia levels, serum glucose, signs of infection, and drug levels (include peak/trough as appropriate). Once acute confusion has been recognized, it is necessary to identify and treat the associated

underlying causes. Complete blood cell count with differential can be helpful in diagnosing infection and anaemia. Glucose levels are assessed to diagnose hypoglycaemia, diabetic ketoacidosis, and hyperosmolar nonketotic states. The calcium-binding protein S-100 B could be a serum marker of delirium. Higher levels

are seen in patients with delirium when compared to patients without delirium.

6. Determine current medications/drug use—especially antianxiety agents, barbiturates, lithium, methyldopa, disulfiram, cocaine, alcohol, amphetamines, hallucinogens, opiates (associated with a high risk of confusion)—and schedule of use as combinations increase risk of adverse reactions/interactions (e.g., cimetidine + antacid, digoxin + diuretics, antacid + propranolol). Medication is one of the most

critical modifiable factors that can cause delirium, especially the use of anticholinergics, antipsychotics, and hypnosedatives. Drugs are a common risk factor for delirium and acute confusion, and drug-induced delirium by medications is commonly seen in medical practice, especially in hospital settings. The risk of

anticholinergic toxicity is greater in older adults, and the risk of inducing delirium by medications is high in frail, older adult patients and in those with dementia.

7. Evaluate the extent of impairment in orientation, attention span, ability to follow directions, send/receive communication, and appropriateness of the response. This should be done to determine the degree of impairment. Patients have difficulty sustaining attention, problems in orientation and short-term memory, poor insight, and impaired judgment. Impaired attention can be assessed with bedside tests that require sustained attention to a task that has not been memorized, such as reciting the days of the week or months of the year backwards, counting backwards from 20, or doing serial subtraction.

8. Note the occurrence/timing of agitation, hallucinations, and violent behaviours. Assess for sundown syndrome. This phenomenon is associated with confusion that occurs in late afternoons. The patient exhibits increasing restlessness, agitation, and confusion. Sundowning may indicate sleep disorders, hunger, thirst, or unmet toileting needs. Sundowning may be triggered by the dimming light and a sense that it's time to change activities or "go home". Evening and darkness may also tap into fears of being unsafe and insecure.

9. Determine whether the patient is experiencing dementia or depression.

Confusion may be present in patients with depression, as well as those who have dementia or delirium. However, because confusion and cognitive difficulties in older adults are so often caused by dementia, care providers usually attribute the patient's confusion to Alzheimer's disease and assume that interventions would be useless.

The Geriatric Depression Scale is especially useful in screening for depression in older adults. It requires minimal training and will help decide whether the patient needs further assessment. See also 11 Geriatric Nursing Care Plans (Older Adult).

10. Assess the patient's level of consciousness. Ask the patient to perform a three-step task. A component of the Mini-Mental Status Examination, this assessment of a three-step task provides a baseline for subsequent assessments of a patient's confusion. A three-step task is complex and is a gross indicator of brain function. Because it requires attention, it can also test for delirium.

11. Assess for pain using a rating scale of 0-10: Acute confusion can be a sign of pain. If the patient is unable to use a scale, assess for behavioural cues such as grimacing, clenched fists, frowning, and hitting. Adequate pain treatment is absolutely crucial to the implementation of this multi-component treatment.

Nursing interventions and rationale

The nursing interventions for managing confusion and delirium aims to manage and treat the underlying cause of confusion, promote patient safety, optimize cognitive function, and educate patients and families on strategies to prevent or manage future episodes of acute confusion.

1. Assist with the treatment of underlying problems (e.g., drug intoxication/substance abuse, infectious process, hypoxemia, biochemical imbalances, nutritional deficits, pain management).

Assisting with the treatment of the underlying problem is important to maximize the level of function and prevent further deterioration. When delirium is diagnosed or suspected, the underlying causes should be sought and treated. Despite every effort, no cause for delirium can be found in a small percentage of patients. Delirium management includes supportive therapy and pharmacological management.

2. Orient the patient to surroundings, staff, and necessary activities as needed. Present reality concisely and briefly. Increased orientation ensures a greater degree of safety for the patient. For most patients, a stay in the hospital is a considerable disruption to their normal way of life. They find themselves in a strange environment, which can result in markedly impaired orientation. Reorientation techniques or memory cues such as calendars, clocks, and family photos may be helpful.

3. Modulate sensory exposure. Provide a calm environment; eliminate extraneous noise and stimuli.

Increased levels of visual and auditory stimulation can be misinterpreted by the confused patient. The environment should be stable, quiet, and well-lighted. One study showed a reduction of sound during the night by using earplugs in the ICU setting decreased the risk of delirium by 53% and improved the self-reported sleep perception of the patient for 48 hours.

4. Encourage family/caregivers to participate in reorientation as well as provide ongoing input (e.g., current news and family happenings). The confused patient may not completely understand what is happening. The presence of family and significant others may enhance the patient's level of comfort. Family members and staff should explain proceedings at every opportunity, reinforce orientation, and reassure the patient. Support from a familiar nurse and family should be encouraged.

5. Give simple directions. Allow sufficient time for the patient to respond, communicate, and make decisions. This communication method can reduce anxiety experienced in a strange environment. It is a good general rule of respectful interaction to correct the patient for mistakes or misunderstandings, however, the nurse should also remember to listen with interest and politeness. Listening will help the nurse determine the depth of confusion, ascertain the wisdom of trying to correct it, and discern that the patient is making sense within a context not immediately evident.

6. Avoid challenging illogical thinking—defensive reactions may result. Challenges to the patient's thinking can be perceived as threatening and result in a defensive reaction. Respect requires that confused patients should always be treated kindly. Spoken correction or redirection should never be condescending but

rather should reflect the gentle authority that gives the patient a sense of security.

7. Provide for safety needs (e.g., supervision, side rails, seizure precautions, placing call bell within reach, positioning needed items within reach/ clearing traffic paths, ambulating with devices). This is to prevent untoward incidents and to promote safety and prevent risk for injury. Simple measures can help minimize confusion and may help prevent falls during the patient's stay in the facility. These measures may include ensuring toilet doors are painted with an identifiable colour, illustrating ward signs with pictures, and ensuring contrast between the floor, bed, and toilet.

8. Avoid the use of restraints. This may worsen the situation and increase the likelihood of untoward complications. Delirious patients may pull out intravenous lines, climb out of bed, and may not be compliant. Perceptual problems lead to agitation, fear, combative behaviour, and wandering. Severely delirious patients benefit from constant

observation or sitters, which may be cost-effective for these patients and help avoid the use of physical restraints. These patients should never be left alone or unattended.

9. Maintain normal fluid and electrolyte balance; establish/maintain normal nutrition, body temperature, oxygenation (if patients experience low oxygen saturation treat with supplemental oxygen), blood glucose levels, and blood pressure. These measures are performed to treat underlying causes of delirium in

collaboration with the health care team. Fluid and nutrition should be given carefully because the patient may be unwilling or physically unable to maintain a balanced intake. For the patient suspected of having alcohol toxicity or alcohol withdrawal, therapy should include multivitamins, especially thiamine.

10. Communicate the patient's status, cognition, and behavioural manifestations to all necessary providers.

Recognize that a patient's fluctuating cognition and behaviour is a hallmark of delirium and is not to be construed as patient preference for caregivers. Safe clinical handover is essential for the delivery of better patient journeys across the entire health system. There is evidence that the poor exchange or delayed sharing of information between health professionals negatively affects the continuity of care.

In turn, this may negatively impact patient outcomes through increased medication errors, higher readmission rates, and unnecessary delays in diagnosis, treatment, and provision of test results.

11. Plan care that allows for an appropriate sleep-wake cycle.

Disturbance in normal sleep and activity patterns should be minimized as those patients with nocturnal exacerbations endure more complications from delirium. Eye masks and earplugs go a long way toward minimizing noise and light exposure in oriented and non-delirious patients, thereby improving sleep quality. Sleep disruption occurs more frequently in hospitals due to nursing and medical interventions, inappropriate lighting, and the failure of patients, visitors, or personnel to adjust the volume of their conversations.

12. Promote decreased caffeine intake.

Decreasing caffeine intake helps to reduce agitation and restlessness. Caffeine overdose can delay sleep onset, reduce total sleep time, change normal sleep stages, and reduce sleep quality. Insufficient sleep or poor sleep quality can at as a risk factor for a variety of diseases, including dementia.

13. Encourage visits by family and friends. Place familiar objects in sight.

An atmosphere that is close to the patient provides orienting clues, maintains an appropriate balance of sensory stimulation, and secures safety. An older patient's confusion and behavioural disturbance can be exacerbated by an unfamiliar environment. Strategies to orient the older patient with confusion can improve their experience. Orientation strategies might include particular signages or the use of colour in the ward area or positioning familiar items around the bed to create a warm and friendly atmosphere where noise and hustle are minimized. Meaningful interactions between the patient and their family members can be ensured by creating a space for caregivers and family members in the facility.

14. Identify self by name at each contact; call the patient by his or her preferred name.

Appropriate communication techniques for patients at risk of confusion. Culture change starts with analysing the individual, team, or organizational practices to identify areas requiring development. Staff needs to listen to the patient, take time to get to know them, and engage with them as equals. Person-centered practice can make a difference in health outcomes and patient satisfaction.

15. Offer reassurance to the patient and use therapeutic communication at frequent intervals.

Patient reassurance and communication are nursing skills that promote trust and orientation and reduce anxiety. The confused patient and their family can become overwhelmed. The experience of delirium in particular is very distressing for the patient. Fear, panic, and anger often arise and they often need counselling and education once the delirium resolves.

16. Identify, evaluate, and treat pain immediately.

Inadequate pain relief is a potential cause of delirium. Pain should be assessed, monitored, and appropriate pain relief should be administered. Opiates can precipitate confusion; therefore, they should be used as clinically appropriate and the patient should be closely monitored after their administration.

17. Provide continuity of care when possible (e.g., provide the same caregivers, avoid room changes). Ensure accurate information is provided during the transfer of care as needed. Continuity of care helps decrease the disorienting effects of hospitalization. Clear, succinct communication is required for all transfers of care, in many cases, electronic communication will be the optimal method. Verbal communication must also occur when follow-up care is required within 48 hours, there is a concern regarding the potential deterioration of a patient, or the patient has complex needs.

18. Assist the family and significant others in developing coping strategies.

The family needs to let the patient do all that he or she is able to do to maximize the patient's level of functioning and quality of life. Provide success-based therapeutic activities based on the patient's preferences, such as music, hobbies, reading, or games, to reduce boredom and frustration, and enhances the quality of life and cognition. Diversional therapy such as the use of rummage boxes is useful for promoting such activities.

19. Teach the family to recognize signs of early confusion and seek medical help.

Early intervention prevents long-term complications. Because delirious patients are often confused and unable to provide accurate information, getting a detailed history from family and caregivers is particularly important. Delirium should always be suspected when a new onset or an acute or subacute deterioration in behaviour, cognition, or function occurs, especially in patients who are older adults, demented or depressed.

20. Ensure that the patient utilizes vision and hearing aids as appropriate.

A simple but indispensable initial measure is to promote vision and hearing with the patient's own glasses and hearing aid. Only then is the patient able to adequately perceive their environment and communicate with the healthcare providers, nurses, and family members. Ensure that the glasses and hearing aids are clean and wellfunctioning.

21. Assist in providing physical and occupational therapy.

Since mobility is restricted during a hospital stay, patients often rapidly lose muscle mass and consequently, muscle strength. The resulting immobility is associated with longer hospital stays and a higher incidence of neuropsychiatric dysfunction. A randomized controlled study demonstrated that early physical and occupational therapy reduces delirium rate from 41 to 28% and significantly increases the likelihood of a return to independent living. Intensive physiotherapy during the daytime also results in physical fatigue and, as a result, a good night's sleep. **22. Ensure avoidance of polypharmacy and intake of over-the-counter medications.**

Many, in particular older adult patients, take multiple medications to treat preexisting diseases. Interactions with the choline, dopamine, or serotonergic system can trigger delirium. A combination of several low-grade delirium-inducing medications can also add to the risk of delirium in the setting of polypharmacy.

Therefore, it is essential to continuously monitor medications and discontinue unnecessary medications in order to prevent delirium.

23. Administer benzodiazepines for patients with drug and substance withdrawal as prescribed.

These agents are reserved for delirium resulting from seizures or withdrawal from alcohol or sedative hypnotics. Benzodiazepines are preferred over neuroleptics for the treatment of delirium resulting from withdrawal. They may also be used when unknown substances may have been ingested and may be helpful in delirium from hallucinogens, cocaine, stimulant, or PCP toxicity. Use special precautions when using benzodiazepines because they may cause respiratory depression, especially for older adult patients.

24. Administer antipsychotics as indicated.

This class of drugs is the medication of choice in the treatment of psychotic symptoms of delirium. If haloperidol is selected, it should be administered in low doses. Administering high-dose haloperidol can result in an overdose and is associated with a greater likelihood of delirium on the following day.

25. Administer melatonin supplements as indicated.

Recent clinical trials showed that the melatonin supplement and its receptor agonist ramelteon may be useful in the prevention and management of delirium and confusion. Melatonin levels were found to be altered in delirium subjects. Melatonin, or Ramelteon can be used for the treatment of insomnia.

26. Provide education and support regarding confusion to the patient and family members.

Provide information on confusion, dementia, and delirium as appropriate including training for the caregiver on how to support the patient. Additional information on services such as support groups, respite services, and other carer support services may be provided to support the caregivers and family members. Be aware of cultural differences among patients and family members; providing information in the

appropriate language of the use of translators may help achieve this goal.

27. Establish a toileting schedule or offer the urinal or bedpan every two hours. Keep the urinal within easy reach.

If the patient has short-term memory problems, toilet or offer the urinal or bedpan every two hours while the patient is awake or every four hours during the night. Establish a toileting schedule and post it on the patient care plan and, inconspicuously, at the bedside. A patient with a short-term memory problem cannot be expected to use the call light, therefore the nurse should place the urinal or bedpan and other essential items within easy reach. A confused patient may wait

until it is too late to seek assistance with toileting.

28. If the patient displays hostile behaviour, avoid arguing with the patient or leave the room if the violence escalates.

Do not argue with a confused patient's interpretation of the environment. State, "I can understand why you may [hear, think, see] that." This approach prevents the escalation of anger in a confused person. If the patient misperceives the nurse's role (e.g. nurse becomes a thief or jailer), leave the room. Return in 15 minutes and reintroduce self to the patient as though it is the first time that the nurse and patient will meet. Patients who are acutely confused have poor short-term memory and may not remember the previous encounter or that the nurse was involved in that encounter.

29. Evaluate the continued need for certain therapies.

Such therapies may become irritating stimuli. If the patient is drinking or eating, consider asking permission to remove the feeding tube. If the patient has an indwelling urethral catheter, discontinue the catheter as indicated and begin a toileting routine.

CHAPTER XI

PSYCHIATRIC CASE MANAGEMENT

One of the most effective comprehensive treatment methods practised in most developed countries is case management.

Definition: It can be defined as a comprehensive biopsychosocial mental health care plan and process in which the team of mental health professionals consisting of psychiatrist, psychiatric nurse, clinical psychologist, psychiatric social worker work together in developing a treatment plan, and produces positive treatment outcomes.

Advantages: All available support systems in a community for mental health are utilized in a coordinated manner by appropriately integrating them with the needs of every individual patient with mental illness. Case management plans overcome many of the complexities that affect effective provision of comprehensive mental health care, rehabilitation, reintegration with family/community for the patient with mental illness and it addresses the rights and responsibilities at all times.

Composition: Members of a case management team Psychiatrist (Clinical team leader), Nurse manager (Case management leader), Psychiatric Nurse, Clinical Psychologist, and Psychiatric Social Worker. The number of the team varies from 5 to 10, usually depending on the caseload that each member can take up at a time. The member delivering case management is called a case manager, and such member keeps strong therapeutic relationships with their clients until desired goals and outcomes of treatment are attained.

Clinical Significance: Case management consists of these six core elements from a clinical perspective.

1.**Patient identification and eligibility determination:** Usually, the clinical and nurse leaders identify and allocate cases to other team members based on patient needs.

2.**Assessment:** The assigned case manager will undertake a detailed, comprehensive understanding of the patient which includes, their healthcare and social needs, their capabilities, and the resources they have access to in their family and community. A biopsychosocial formulation is done and discussed with the team.

3.**Care planning:** This process is done in discussion with the team, taking inputs, knowledge, and expertise from the team leaders. The desired treatment goals, therapeutic actions to achieve them, specific services and supports required to achieve the stated goals and finally, the identification of targeted outcomes that are specific to the patient/patient. Navigation encompasses the part of the case management process where the case manager helps guide the patient/patient to services and supports recognizing and working to remove barriers that can either be anticipated or those that unexpectedly arise. Provision of care occurs when the case manager is also part of the treatment team, as might happen in the mental health setting. For example, the patient's case manager might also be part of the therapy team, providing counselling and skills training.

4.Plan implementation: Implementation is the part of the case management program where the plan of care, with its varied activities and tasks, is set in motion. Coordination is related to navigation but is broader and refers to the myriads of facilitations that must occur between and among care providers, service settings, organizations, and institutions, with the patient/patient also being the focus and at

the centre of this component of the case management process.

5.Plan monitoring: Monitoring occurs throughout the entire process and is related to seeking ongoing feedback and conducting follow-up as necessary on how the plan of care is being implemented and producing results. Evaluation is closely process to formally determine if the care plan helps the patient/patient achieve progress towards goals and outcomes. Feedback as a component of case

management involves communication with service providers about their services' effectiveness. It supports assisting the patient/patient in making progress as defined in the plan of care. Providing education and information encompasses helping the patient/patient and their family/support system develop a deeper understanding of relevant health and healthcare topics. Advocacy refers to activities directed at empowering the patient/patient to pursue services and supports, related accommodations, and proper entitlements to their circumstances. Supportive counselling describes the case manager's effort to consistently provide encouragement and emotional support as the care plan unfolds. Administration

encompasses the paperwork, report writing, and data gathering and analysis that are part and parcel of the modern healthcare system.

6. Transition and discharge: Transition describes the process when a patient is prepared to move across the healthcare continuum, depending on the patient's health and the need for services. The patient can be moved home or transferred to another facility for further care. Discharge represents the case management process component in which the patient's/ patient's case reaches the point of closure, goals are met, and the patient's needs warrant disengagement with the case management process. Finally, community service development occurs when the case management process uncovers a need or service gap within a given community. Then, the case manager catalyzes efforts to create that service or support to fill that gap.

Conclusion: The case management process fundamentally assists a specific patient/patient in coordinating and navigating through their healthcare journey. The key to this assistance is the construction and implementation of a relevant and feasible plan of care that, when followed, will help the patient move towards their stated goals and positive health outcomes with an optimal level of functional capability, wellness, and self-management. Case management will ultimately improve the quality of life for

the patient.

As we conclude the 'Clinical Guide of Psychiatric Nursing', I hope this book has provided valuable insights, practical strategies, and compassionate approaches to caring for patients with psychiatric conditions. Psychiatric nursing requires clinical knowledge, patience, empathy, and resilience.

Every interaction with a patient is an opportunity to offer comfort, stability, and hope. Your role as a caregiver extends beyond treatment—building trust, fostering healing, and advocating for those who may not always have a voice.

I appreciate your dedication to psychiatric nursing. May this guide continue to support you in providing safe, effective, and compassionate care.

Stay committed. Stay compassionate. Stay inspired.